Sex, Personal Relationships and the Law for Adults with Learning Disabilities

A guide to decision making in England and Wales, including the Mental Capacity Act (2005) and Sexual Offences Act (2003)

David Thompson

Pavilion

Sex, Personal Relationships and the Law for Adults with Learning Disabilities

A guide to decision making in England and Wales, including the Mental Capacity Act (2005) and Sexual Offences Act (2003)

Published by:
Pavilion Publishing and Media Ltd
Rayford House
School Road
Hove
East Sussex
BN3 5HX
Tel: 01273 434 943
Fax: 01273 227 308
Email: info@pavpub.com

Published 2018

A catalogue record for this book is available from the British Library.

ISBN: 978-1-911028-88-8

Pavilion is the leading training and development provider and publisher in the health, social care and allied fields, providing a range of innovative training solutions underpinned by sound research and professional values. We aim to put our customers first, through excellent customer service and value.

Author: David Thompson
Production editor: Ruth Chalmers, Pavilion Publishing and Media Ltd
Cover design: Tony Pitt, Pavilion Publishing and Media Ltd
Page layout and typesetting: Emma Dawe, Pavilion Publishing and Media Ltd
Printing: CMP Digital Print Solutions

Contents

About this book iv

About the author v

Acknowledgements v

Introduction..1

Chapter 1: The sexual experiences of people with learning disabilities..............11

Chapter 2: Consent to sex under the Mental Capacity Act (2005) 19

Chapter 3: Decisions concerning contraception, sterilisation
and pregnancy under the Mental Capacity Act (2005) 49

Chapter 4: The Sexual Offences Act (2003) 65

Chapter 5: Marriage, civil partnership and forced marriages...............................77

References and resources...89

Appendix: Guidance for decision-making for a pregnant woman
who may lack capacity to make decisions about her
antenatal, perinatal and postnatal care...93

About this book

This book explains how law and policy should inform support for adults with learning disabilities in matters related to sex and relationships. This covers how to decide if a person with learning disabilities can consent to a current sexual relationship, and what response is required depending on the outcome of this assessment. It also explores consent issues related to marriage, civil partnerships and the control of procreation.

The book focuses on the law in England and Wales only, as these countries share the legislation most related to the capacity to consent to sex – particularly the Sexual Offences Act (2003) (SOA) and the Mental Capacity Act (2005). Where legislation differs between these two countries, this is identified.

Information is given about key cases that have gone to court prior to the publication of this book. The judgements from these cases need to inform responses to people with learning disabilities in similar situations. As such, readers need to be alert to subsequent cases in the courts that may require changes to practice.

The intended audience for this book is those who work with people with learning disabilities. However, the legislation discussed equally applies to other individuals where there may be concerns about their ability to consent to sex and relationships. This includes people with dementia, brain injury or mental health needs.

This guide aims to help structure decision-making by services. It does not set out how to work with individuals with learning disabilities directly – whether through sex education, counselling or therapy. However, it does include suggested resources for such work. This includes *Sex and the 3 Rs,* which was recently revised by Michelle McCarthy and the author (Pavilion Publishing, 2016).

Readers are encouraged to read the introductory chapter, which provides an overview of the key legislation and in what situations each should apply. Chapter 1, which looks at the sexual experiences of people with learning disabilities, is included to ensure that support is informed by the research in this area. Individual chapters can then be consulted to provide more detailed guidance on how the law should be applied in specific situations. The case examples included in these later chapters are intended to help illustrate how the law should be practically applied.

About the author

David Thompson has had a diverse career in health and social care, covering direct work, research, policy and practice development. After training to be a teacher of children with learning disabilities, he spent over 10 years providing sex education to people with learning disabilities. This work was the focus of his PhD. He subsequently broadened his interests in the lives of people with learning disabilities to include ageing, support for family carers and advocacy. He was heavily involved in the implementation of the Mental Capacity Act (2005) for the Department of Health in England, which included developing the Independent Mental Capacity Advocate role for the Deprivation of Liberty Safeguards. Before relocating to Australia with his civil partner in 2016, he was vice-chair of the Ann Craft Trust.

Acknowledgements

My involvement with people with learning disabilities on sexual issues was inspired by attending a workshop led by Ann Craft. Craft pioneered work which respected people with learning disabilities as having sexual feelings, desires and rights. After her premature death, I was honoured to serve on the management committee of the Ann Craft Trust. In this role, I was asked to run a course in Nottingham on sex and the law. This book is based on the materials for this course, which I further developed and delivered as the Safeguarding Adults Nurse at Hounslow and Richmond Community NHS Trust.

I would also like to acknowledge Michelle McCarthy, Reader at the Tizard Centre, with whom I have collaborated over many years. She has consistently identified how power, particularly relating to gender, impacts on the personal lives of people with learning disabilities.

Introduction

My work with people with learning disabilities on sexual issues started over 25 years ago. Naturally, many of the individuals I worked with wanted to have or were having relationships and sex. The challenge I found was to identify how best to offer support, together with when and how to intervene if there were concerns about abuse. This challenge continues, but the context of this work has changed enormously. For example, I began in institutions housing hundreds of people with learning disabilities, which no longer exist. At that time, these individuals were supposedly protected by a law which forbade sex with 'mental defectives', and no one in a same-sex relationship had the opportunity to get married.

While there have been many positive developments in policy and law, it is not necessarily true that the opportunities for people with learning disabilities to have relationships and sex have consistently improved. Having regular contact with many people with learning disabilities may increase the chances of finding a boyfriend or girlfriend (with learning disabilities) and allows relationships to develop. However, policy has largely directed people with learning disabilities to spend less time together, for example, through the closure of many large residential units and day centres.

Many people with learning disabilities therefore only spend time with other people with learning disabilities if they happen to attend the same service – whether this be residential, day, educational, employment or social. If people wish to develop an intimate relationship, these very often happen at services they share.

Being limited to forming and conducting relationships in these constraining circumstances can be problematic for a number of reasons. For example, a day centre's or college's toilets may be the most private space available for many couples with learning disabilities, and therefore become the only place that sexual experiences can take place. However inappropriate others may think this is, it needs to be asked whether the individuals realistically have anywhere else to go.

Support for individuals to meet friends or partners outside of shared services is rare. This is often because carers (both paid and family) do not prioritise finding out about which relationships are most important to the person they care for, or find it difficult to find the time to facilitate meetings. There may also be ambivalence, fear or even hostility about individuals having relationships and what these might lead to. Too many residential service providers only arrange contact with other people with learning disabilities when it is someone's birthday, which will often involve inviting just the people living in other services in the same organisation, rather than taking the time to find out who the individual would actually like to attend. People living in the large residential services of the past, in contrast, could often make their own arrangements to meet up, without the need for staff support or transport. While relationships could flourish in such settings, so did sexual abuse (McCarthy & Thompson, 1996).

The development of friendship and dating agencies for people with learning disabilities, in some ways, meets a need created by policy changes which have left people with learning disabilities more isolated from each other.

It should not be assumed that people with learning disabilities will want relationships only with other people with learning disabilities. Indeed, some people with learning disabilities are explicit about seeking relationships elsewhere. Policies which have led people with learning disabilities to increasingly live in their own homes with control over their own money have given individuals more space to develop such relationships. There may be limited awareness of these relationships or interference by others. As with all relationships, these opportunities may offer joy and contentment, but can also be exploitative.

In addition to the risk of sexual abuse, individuals with learning disabilities living alone can be targets for financial exploitation. This includes cases where the relationship is a front for a partner to move into the person's property. People with learning disabilities are not alone in potentially being more attractive partners because they have money or somewhere nice to live. One cultural stereotype, for example, is of relatively young women moving in with wealthy older men. This isn't necessarily exploitation – and if it is, who is abusing who?

While the sexual opportunities and experiences of many people with learning disabilities have been influenced by changes in policy and law, this may be less so for the majority who continue to live with their families. Families hold very diverse views about relationships informed by culture and religion. For example, attitudes to same-sex relations have generally become more positive. This has made it easier for some lesbian or gay men with learning disabilities to 'come out' to their families. Families may also have specific views on relationships involving people with learning disabilities. For example, some parents would not want their child to get married. Other parents may expect and facilitate this through an arranged or forced marriage.

The above illustrates the evolving and varied context in which people with learning disabilities have sex and relationships. The intention of this introduction is not to debate the merits of changes in law, policy and practice, but to identify the powerful influence they have on the lives of people with learning disabilities. This includes their effect on vulnerability and responses to sexual abuse. What has not changed is the risk of sexual abuse closely following opportunities for sexual relationships – from the grounds of the large institutions since closed, to the 'supported living' flats more common today. This book addresses the tension between supporting relationships and trying to prevent and respond to sexual abuse. The legislation provides a critical structure to support services' decision-making in this area.

The legislation in England and Wales

The key legislation in England and Wales explained in this book is set out below. Where this legislation also applies to other parts of the United Kingdom this is noted. Thus, specific sections are also relevant in Northern Ireland and Scotland.

The Mental Capacity Act (2005)

The major focus of this book is how the Mental Capacity Act (2005) applies to the personal lives of people with learning disabilities. The act applies across England and Wales. Since its implementation in 2007, services and professionals have gradually come to understand how central this law needs to be in informing how people should – and sometimes must – be supported. The Mental Capacity Act Code of Practice (2005) provides guidance on how to apply the legislation. It has statutory force, which means that those who work with people with learning disabilities need to have regard for what it says. Any decision not to follow this guidance could be tested in the courts.

The Mental Capacity Act (2005) only applies to individuals who are over the age of 16 who may lack capacity to make specific decisions. Not all parts apply to young adults between the ages of 16 and 18. It is highlighted in the text where this is the case. The distinct legal framework for decision-making for children across England and Wales is largely set out in the Children's Act (1989).

The Mental Capacity Act (2005) is inclusive of people who may temporarily lack capacity to make a decision, for example, because they are drunk, and those with a more permanent condition which may affect decision-making. In addition to people with learning disabilities, this includes people with dementia, brain injury or mental health needs.

The Mental Capacity Act (2005) established the Court of Protection. This is a specialist court which makes decisions regarding individuals who may be unable to make decisions themselves. Judgements made about individuals by the Court of Protection should inform responses to people with learning disabilities in similar situations. For example, the Court of Protection has provided guidance on how to assess for capacity to consent to sex – guidance which was not part of the original legislation. Included are the key judgements made up until late 2017 when this book was completed. There will be further judgements made which will need to inform and possibly change practice. For this reason, services need to watch for further cases, including any which are appealed to a higher court (see the Resources section of this book for links to websites that publish judgements of court cases across the UK).

Deprivation of Liberty Safeguards

In 2008 the Mental Capacity Act (2005) was amended to include the Deprivation of Liberty Safeguards. The aim was to ensure the governments of England and Wales met their responsibilities under Article 5 of the Human Rights Act (1998). Article 5 states: 'Everyone has the right to liberty and security of person. No one shall be deprived of his or her liberty [unless] in accordance with a procedure prescribed in law'.

The Deprivation of Liberty Safeguards can provide a legal basis to deprive a person with a learning disability of their liberty outside of the criminal justice system or the Mental Health Act (1983). The safeguards can be relevant where it is thought to be in the best interests of a person with learning disabilities to restrict contact with individuals who may put them at sexual risk or who they could themselves sexually abuse – if the restrictions in effect deprive the person of their liberty.

The Deprivation of Liberty Safeguards have been much criticised, and there are already plans to replace them (Law Commission, 2017). Regardless of this, services for people with learning disabilities often have great power and control over individuals, including their sexual lives. The Deprivation of Liberty Safeguards can provide an important safeguard to protect against potentially arbitrary restrictions. This includes restrictions to the rights of people with learning disabilities to 'private and family life', under Article 8 of the Human Rights Act (1998).

The Mental Capacity Act in Northern Ireland

The Mental Capacity Act (Northern Ireland) (2016) has many similarities to the Mental Capacity Act (2005). This includes the requirement to support people to make their own decisions wherever possible, to act in the best interests of individuals who have been assessed as lacking capacity to make a decision, and additional safeguards where there may be a deprivation of a person's liberty. The detail is different to the legislation in England and Wales. This, together with the act's very recent implementation, are the reasons why it is not covered in this book.

The Sexual Offences Act (2003)

The Sexual Offences Act (2003) applies across England and Wales. Parts of it also apply in Northern Ireland and, to a lesser extent, Scotland. These two countries have their own distinct legislation, covering, for example, sex involving the abuse of a professional relationship, or taking advantage of an adult's vulnerability because of their learning disability (Sexual Offences (Northern Ireland) Order (2008) & Sexual Offences Act (Scotland) (2009)). Therefore, the chapter in this book on the Sexual Offences Act (2003) (Chapter 4) should not be used as a resource for Northern Ireland or Scotland.

Essentially, the Sexual Offences Act (2003) provides a list of sexual offences. The potential consequences for perpetrators if they are found guilty of one or more of these offences are set out, including maximum prison sentences. The list includes offences against children and adults, which may be committed by children or adults.

The Sexual Offences Act (2003) replaced the outdated Sexual Offences Act (1956). This, for example, made it illegal for a man to have sex with a woman who was a 'defective'. A defective was defined by the Mental Health Act (1959) as someone 'suffering from severe subnormality'. The act excluded a whole group of people from having sex, without paying attention to any individual's capacity to consent. Fortunately, when the current Sexual Offences Act (2003) was developed, there was considerable consultation with those working with people with learning disabilities on sexual issues. This included Ann Craft and to a lesser extent myself. As a consequence, the act tried to be sensitive to sexual exploitation and abuse as it was known to affect people with learning disabilities, while not criminalising consensual relationships. As will be seen in Chapter 1, which is titled 'The sexual experiences of people with learning disabilities', there can be a very fine line between these.

Using the Mental Capacity Act (2005) or the Sexual Offences Act 2003

The Mental Capacity Act (2005) must be used to inform decisions about how to support adults with learning disabilities who may be involved in sexual relationships, including decisions about whether those relationships could be exploitative or abusive. The act needs to be understood as the fundamental practice guide for all services working with adults with learning disabilities. Workers should reflect frequently on whether an individual has capacity to make their own decisions, and if not, must ensure decisions are made in the person's best interests. The act must guide, for example, services' responses to the following decisions:

■ whether to inform a parent, against a man with learning disabilities' wishes, about his sexual relationship with another man

■ how to respond to a woman with learning disabilities who wants to have her boyfriend spend the night with her

■ whether to stop a man with learning disabilities accessing pornography

■ whether to increase supervision of a man with learning disabilities to minimise the risk of him touching women inappropriately or abusively

■ whether a woman with learning disabilities should use a contraceptive, and if so, which type

■ how to respond to a man with learning disabilities who wants to wear women's clothes.

In comparison, the Sexual Offences Act (2003) only applies if a sexual crime may have been committed. This includes sexual exploitation or abuse committed either against or by a person with learning disabilities. The act should inform decisions as to whether the police should be contacted where there is some concerning sexual activity involving a person with learning disabilities. Examples include:

■ a woman with learning disabilities potentially being financially and sexually abused by a man without learning disabilities

■ a staff member suspected of having a sexual relationship with a person with learning disabilities

■ a man with learning disabilities masturbating in public

■ a man with learning disabilities grabbing the breasts of female staff members

■ a man with learning disabilities talking about his father having sex with him when he was a child

■ a man with learning disabilities having sex with a man with more severe learning disabilities.

There are differences between how an individual's ability to consent to sex is determined in the Mental Capacity Act (2005) and in the Sexual Offences Act (2003). Essentially, the Mental Capacity Act (2005) looks at a person's knowledge and understanding of sex. While this is also critical in the Sexual Offences Act (2003), consideration is also given to whom a person with learning disabilities is having sex with to decide if a crime has been committed. For example, irrespective of a person with learning disabilities' knowledge of sex or willingness to participate, it is illegal for staff members to have sex with them. Further, the Sexual Offences Act (2003) recognises the potential vulnerability of some adults who have the capacity to consent to sex. Case law has identified that such individuals may potentially be unable to resist having sex with specific people out of fear or what might happen, even if direct threats are not made. That is, they may have capacity to consent to sex with some people but not others. This is explained in greater detail in Chapter 4.

Civil partnership, marriage and forced marriage

In common with the wider population, many people with learning disabilities desire to have their relationships recognised by the institutions of marriage and civil partnership. The final chapters of this book explore consent to civil partnerships and marriage.

Civil partnerships were introduced for same-sex couples across the UK by the Civil Partnership Act (2004). The Marriage (Same Sex Couples) Act (2013) subsequently legalised same-sex marriage in England and Wales. Similar legislation was passed in Scotland the following year (the Marriage and Civil Partnership (Scotland) Act (2014)). Irrespective of these steps towards equality, the option for couples to enter civil partnerships continues to exist, but controversially only for same-sex couples. Northern Ireland is unique in not allowing same-sex marriage. It treats same-sex couples married elsewhere in the UK as being in a civil partnership.

The assessments of capacity to either marry or enter into a civil partnership are not covered by the Mental Capacity Act (2005). These assessments are essentially the responsibility of the official conducting the ceremony, and different criteria apply for each. These are found in the Civil Partnership Act (2004) and case law concerning marriage dating from the Marriage Act of (1753). Where a marriage or civil partnership has taken place, concerns about the ability of one person to have freely consented to this can be referred to the courts, with the potential of invalidating the contract.

There has been a growing recognition of marriages where one person either did not give their consent or was not able to give consent. Very often these marriages involve people with learning disabilities and people moving to the UK to gain residency. The section on forced marriage, in Chapter 5, provides information about what should be done where there are concerns about a person with learning disabilities potentially entering, or who may already be in, a forced marriage. This includes the provisions of the Anti-social Behaviour, Crime and Policing Act (2014), which, for example, makes it a criminal offence to marry someone who lacks the capacity to consent to marriage, whether or not they have been pressured to do so.

Is there a requirement to report potential sexual abuse of or abusing by a person with learning disabilities?

If a sexual crime has possibly been committed involving a person with learning disabilities, then a decision may need to be made on whether to involve the police. There is currently no legal requirement to report potential sexual crimes involving either adults or children (whether or not they have learning disabilities) to the police.

There is a strong expectation in England (Children's Act (2004)) and a requirement in Wales (Social Services and Well-being (Wales) Act (2014)) to report concerns about the welfare of a child under the age of 18 to the local authority. These reporting requirements are relevant if, for example, a man with learning disabilities is alleged to have touched a child sexually.

Local authorities are required to ensure the potential abuse or neglect of adults with learning disabilities is investigated in England (Care Act (2015)) and Wales (Social Services and Well-being (Wales) Act (2014)). There is a significant difference in that in Wales there is a duty to report actual or potential abuse of an adult with learning disabilities to the local authorities, whereas in England reporting is generally expected, but not required.

Where the law allows a decision about reporting potential sexual crimes to the police, or sexual abuse to the local authority, the Mental Capacity Act (2005) should be used to inform such decisions. For example, if there are concerns that a woman with learning disabilities is being sexually abused by a man without learning disabilities, reports could be made to both the police and social services. Following the Mental Capacity Act (2005), an early consideration must be whether the women herself is able to make the decision about reporting. If she has the capacity to make this decision, she could reasonably decide that she doesn't want any interference in her private life, even if she acknowledges elements of abuse in the relationship (an 'unwise' decision allowed under the act). This decision may need to be respected. If the woman is assessed as lacking capacity to make a decision about reporting, this can be done in her best interests.

The legal duty for people who work with people with learning disabilities to have 'regard' for the Mental Capacity Act Code of Practice (2005) gives space for some discretion. So, in the example above, the police could be informed about the potential abuse even if the woman has capacity to decide otherwise. It could be argued that 'regard' has been given to the woman's capacity to make her own decision, but the police have been involved because of concerns about the welfare of other people with learning disabilities. This might be the case if the man is thought to develop deliberately exploitative relationships with women with learning disabilities. This justification might need to be defended against any claim by the woman or her advocates that her rights to 'private and family life' under Article 8 of the Human Rights Act (1998), or even confidentiality under the Data Protection Act (1998), have been breached.

One case in the Court of Protection has suggested professionals have a responsibility to report suspected abuse of people with learning disabilities (XCC v AA & Others [2012] EWHC 2183 (COP)). Here the judge was very critical of three doctors who did not report the abuse of a women with severe learning disabilities. They had been asked by family members to provide support around pregnancy, despite the court finding that it was 'obvious' she lacked capacity to make decisions about sex and marriage.

Female genital mutilation

Female genital mutilation (FGM) is one type of abuse where there are mandatory reporting requirements across England and Wales. Regulated health and social care professionals and teachers must advise the police if they learn or see evidence that a girl under the age of 18 has suffered FGM. This is set out under Section 5B of the Female Genital Mutilation Act (2003), which came into force on 31 October 2015. This duty to report does not extend to women over the age of 18 who were mutilated as children. The Home Office has produced guidance in this area (2016).

Chapter 1: The sexual experiences of people with learning disabilities

The introduction of this book suggested that there has been a move towards acceptance of people with learning disabilities having sex and relationships. While this may be the case generally, individuals with learning disabilities can face very different responses from family members, carers and professionals to any knowledge of their sexual lives. These responses are variously informed by:

- beliefs in the rights of people with learning disabilities to have sex and relationships

- values – possibly cultural – about sexual relationships, generally or specifically, involving people with learning disabilities

- concerns about the vulnerability of people with learning disabilities to sexual abuse

- an understanding of the law.

What is often missing is an understanding of how people with learning disabilities may experience sex and relations. This includes the sexual activities that could take place and how these activities feel to the people experiencing them. Perhaps we don't want to know this because it is considered too private? Alternatively, romantic assumptions may be made about sex being mutually pleasurable.

If we don't know how people with learning disabilities experience sex, we risk ill-informed responses, including a failure to respond. For example, I was asked to support a service that was often 'turning a blind eye' to a man with learning disabilities taking a less able man with learning disabilities to the bathroom, where it was understood they had sex. There were lots of reasons to be worried about the contact because:

- the less able man had extremely limited verbal communication

- the more able man frequently intimidated other people with learning disabilities

- the more able man led the other to the bathroom

- the two men did not socialise with each other outside of the bathroom.

It was suggested that the less able man was agreeable to the contact because he didn't resist going to the bathroom. There was little consideration given to how difficult it would have been for him to resist when the other man was known to be intimidating, or to how 'learnt compliance' – which has been a feature of the lives of too many people with learning disabilities – may have undermined any potential protest.

What was known outside of the bathroom provided more than enough grounds for the service to stop the contact and to report a potential sexual crime. Indeed, one reason the more able man had rarely been stopped from taking the other man to the bathroom was because many staff members were afraid of how he might respond to them.

What was happening in the bathroom? Is it possible to make assumptions from the 'relationship' outside about the sex taking place inside? The most likely picture was of the more able man doing what he wanted to the other man. This was depressingly confirmed when I was asked to work with the more able man. He described anally penetrating the other man, without any lubrication and with an awareness of the other man's pain and distress.

The above is an extreme example, but it does show how negligent services can be at times to the potential sexual abuse of people with learning disabilities. It also requires us to be realistic about the nature of any sexual contact based on what is known about the individuals involved and their relationship, in order to inform any response.

Findings from research

Rarely have people with learning disabilities been asked explicitly about their sexual lives. This is a very private area for everyone, so there are good reasons to be cautious about doing so. In my early sex education work with people with learning disabilities it felt important to understand how sex was experienced to inform how best to offer support. For example, when providing safer sex work with a man having sex with men, knowing if he anally penetrated other men, was anally penetrated himself or didn't have anal sex was essential information. This would inform whether I should prioritise teaching him to put a condom on himself or how to encourage his partners to use them. But this teaching could still have been very misguided if, as was often the case, he described being anally penetrated as being very painful and seemed powerless to do anything other than 'wait until it finished'.

My colleague at that time was Michelle McCarthy, who was committed to empowering women with learning disabilities in their sexual relationships.

Together we documented what women and men with learning disabilities were telling us about their sexual lives in the context of the sex education support we were providing. This was developed into several research publications (see, for example, McCarthy, 1999; Thompson, 2001).

A summary of this research is provided here. It identifies how sex is most commonly experienced by people with learning disabilities, whether or not their sexual partner also has a learning disability.

Sex involving a woman and a man

- Choices about what sex takes place are overwhelmingly made by the man. The woman's control may be limited to resisting specific activities.

- In addition to penetrative vaginal sex, there is often penetrative anal sex.

- Women experience vaginal and anal sex on a scale between uncomfortable and painful.

- Women intensely dislike having the man's penis in their mouth.

- Both men and women have a greater knowledge of men's orgasms than women's. Women rarely or never have orgasms.

- Sex ends with the man's orgasm or him giving up trying to have one.

- Women are in a very poor position to insist on contraception or other protective measures.

Sex involving two men

- The more intellectually able man will control what happens. He makes choices designed to maximise his own sexual pleasure: doing what he wants to the other man, or getting him to do what he wants.

- It is very unlikely to be a mutually enjoyed sexual experience – with, for example, both men having orgasms. At best the men might 'take turns' to do what they want to the other man.

- When it happens, being penetrated anally is experienced as painful. (It doesn't have to be with a sensitive partner and lubricant.)

- It is unrealistic to expect the less powerful man to be able to negotiate safe sex, for example, to get the other man to use a condom.

- Men with learning disabilities have sex with men at a similar frequency to men with learning disabilities having sex with women. Some more able men with learning disabilities will have sex with both women and men if the opportunities are available.

Sex between two women

■ Women with learning disabilities extremely rarely have sex with women. Their common lack of knowledge about their bodies' potential for sexual pleasure and orgasms is a factor in this.

■ Because of how rare this is, it is difficult to generalise about such women's sexual experiences, but one woman may be controlling what sex takes place.

The patterns presented above were very consistent, but this does not deny the possibility of individuals having very different experiences. It is clearly a very negative picture and needs further consideration in order to understand why so many people with learning disabilities were involved in sex which offered little or no sexual pleasure.

Michelle McCarthy identified a number of reasons why women with learning disabilities were not complaining about their sexual experiences with men. Generally, this was with men who they believed were, or hoped to be, their boyfriends – even if this wasn't the man's view or intention. She found that women with learning disabilities believed the following:

■ To be valued it is necessary to have a boyfriend or get married.

■ Sex is something that women have to do in order to get or keep a boyfriend.

■ Sex is something that men enjoy.

■ Sex isn't something that women should expect to enjoy.

So while the women may not have enjoyed the physical experience of sex (often putting up with uncomfortable or painful penetrative sex) they may have gained pleasure from the sex reinforcing positive feelings about being in a relationship. This picture is not unique to women with learning disabilities. The feminist movement has for a long time challenged women's experiences, including their sexual experiences, in heterosexual relationships.

The summary above is based on research which took place 20 years ago. The question needs to be asked whether things have changed significantly for people with learning disabilities. There has been limited further research, but unfortunately, this work suggests that little has changed. For example, in 2015 Lou Townson wrote of her interviews with women with learning disabilities:

Many of the women talked about their own relationships with men and partners. Some of the women didn't realise that what they were experiencing was actually abuse; they had assumed it was a natural part of a relationship.' (Chapman *et al*, 2015: p164)

Research into 'mate crime' involving people with learning disabilities provides further evidence. Rob Landman, who has studied this area, presents this bluntly:

'The primacy of the relationship can be more important than what's happening inside it. People are prepared to put up with all sorts of crap to keep a relationship that may be the only one they have apart from with someone who's being paid to be with them.' (quoted in Williams, 2010)

Sexual behaviour and identity

The growing acceptance in society of same-sex relationships has to some extent been reflected in the lives of people with learning disabilities. There are now rare examples of men with learning disabilities entering civil partnerships and getting married. One of the most important studies in this area is the work of David Abbott and Joyce Howarth, entitled *Secret Loves, Hidden Lives* (2005). It describes the challenges faced by lesbian, gay and bisexual people with learning disabilities when 'coming out', as well as in finding and developing relationships.

This work also found same-sex relationships involving women with learning disabilities to be rare compared to those involving men with learning disabilities. However, extreme isolation from other lesbians and gay men was a common experience for both women and men with learning disabilities. The study also highlighted the vulnerability of men with learning disabilities to exploitation and abuse in their sexual relationships with other men, including those who may not have a learning disability. *Richard's story* is a very illustrative film about one gay men with learning disabilities (www.scie.org.uk/lgbtqi/video-stories/learning-disabilities).

Traditionally, same-sex relationships involving men with learning disabilities have been explained away as a consequence of restricted sexual opportunities with women. The term 'institutional homosexuality' is unhelpful, as it disregards the reasons for men's participation. This could be because they want sex with other men (whether or not they want sex with women), or they are being sexually abused.

Services should not label the sexuality of people with learning disabilities. It is up to each individual whether they choose to identify as lesbian, gay, bisexual or heterosexual, and it is acceptable not to take any of these identities. As in the wider population, for example, not every man who enjoys sex with other men sees themselves as being gay. Also, there continues to be considerable prejudice against sexualities other than heterosexuality, which prevents many people from declaring a different sexual identity.

Case example: Shirley

Shirley is a participant in a sex education group for women with learning disabilities. She lives in her own flat with staff support a few hours a week. She talks about her 'boyfriend' Ray, who visits her at home about once a week. Often, they will have sex when he visits. She describes him sometimes 'doing the front or back', which the group facilitator confirms to be penetrative vaginal and anal sex. Shirley says this 'hurts', but she lets him do it because she is his 'girlfriend'. She says he has tried to put his penis in her mouth but she thinks this is 'horrible' so won't let him.

Shirley has a limited understanding of sexually transmitted diseases. She knows people can get AIDS if they have sex, but does not relate this to the sex she has with Ray. She is not worried that condoms are not being used. She also says she won't get pregnant because she is too old (she is 54). Shirley is clear she doesn't want anyone else to know what happens with Ray.

How should the group facilitator respond?

From what is known about Shirley's sexual relationship, the facilitator could reasonably try to help her be more assertive. This might include ensuring she knows about female orgasms and helping her make positive choices about any sex she has with Ray. In practice, it could be very difficult for Shirley to change the nature of the sex or the relationship. Ultimately, it may be about her choice to continue to put up with how sex happens to maintain the relationship, or to end it.

Chapter 2 on the Mental Capacity Act (2005) would suggest that Shirley has capacity to consent to sex. If this is the case, the facilitator or services need to take care not to make decisions in Shirley's 'best interests' that she is able to make herself.

A crime is potentially being committed under the Sexual Offences Act (2003). This would be the case if Ray was a staff member. It could also be true if Ray was deliberately taking advantage of Shirley's learning disabilities, for example, if he was promising her that they would get married in order to gain her compliance to sex when he had no intention of doing so.

The facilitator needs to be clear on why there may be grounds to break Shirley's request for confidentiality. The section in the introduction titled 'Is there a requirement to report potential sexual abuse?' explains that there is no duty for professionals to report potential crimes. However, under safeguarding adults' legislation, in Wales there is a requirement and in England an expectation to report suspected abuse of people with learning disabilities. Advice here would be to override Shirley's reasonable wishes for privacy if a sexual crime was suspected, but not to if the main concern was insensitivity in the relationship. If the latter were the case, ideally Ray would receive input to educate and challenge him about his sexual relationships with women.

What should sex education cover?

Knowing how people with learning disabilities commonly experience sex should set the agenda for the content of general sex education. Ideally, for both women and men it should include:

- information about women's orgasms and how they can be achieved

- positive representations of same-sex relationships and sex

- the expectation of sex being physically pleasurable to both people involved

- information about anal sex

- information about how lubricant can be accessed and used

- the right to have preferences about sexual acts and to say no to specific ones

- paying attention to the other person's experience of sex – for example, who is enjoying it most and why?

- identifying and challenging insensitive, exploitative and abusive sexual behaviour.

If people with learning disabilities are not exposed to these ideas, through either informal or formal learning, there can be little optimism of a more positive picture of their sexual experiences in another 20 years.

Chapter 2: Consent to sex under the Mental Capacity Act (2005)

The Mental Capacity Act (2005) was first implemented in 2007. It filled a gap in the legislation about how decisions (other than financial) should be made if there are concerns about an individual's ability to make decisions themselves. It applies across England and Wales.

There are five underlying principles of the Mental Capacity Act (2005). These must guide all work with adults with learning disabilities, whether or not an individual has capacity to make a specific decision. Table 2.1 reproduces the five principles as written in the Mental Capacity Act Code of Practice. Alongside each principle is a description of what it means specifically in relation to sexual decisions for people with learning disabilities.

Table 2.1: The five principles of the Mental Capacity Act (2005) and how they relate to sexual decisions for people with learning disabilities	
Principle	In relation to sexual decisions for people with learning disabilities
1. A person must be assumed to have capacity unless it is established that they lack capacity.	It should be assumed that people with learning disabilities are able to consent to sex.
2. A person is not to be treated as unable to make a decision unless all practicable steps to help them do so have been taken without success.	People with learning disabilities should be provided with sex education.
3. A person is not to be treated as unable to make a decision merely because they make an unwise decision.	People with learning disabilities may choose to have or stay in relationships which other people may consider as exploitative or abusive.

Principle	In relation to sexual decisions for people with learning disabilities
4. An act done, or decision made, under this act for or on behalf of a person who lacks capacity must be done, or made, in their best interests.	People with learning disabilities must first be assessed as lacking capacity to consent to sex if any decisions are to be made in their best interests.
5. Before the act is done, or the decision is made, regard must be given to whether the purpose for which it is needed can be as effectively achieved in a way that is less restrictive of the person's rights and freedom of action.	Where a person with learning disabilities lacks capacity to consent to sex, it is not always in their best interests to stop them having sex.

Assuming adults with learning disabilities can consent to sex

The first principle indicates that we must start from the assumption that adults with learning disabilities are able to have sexual relationships. Adults with learning disabilities are not required to first prove that they can consent to sex before being 'allowed' to have sexual relationships. Instead, those who support people with learning disabilities should only intervene if they can show that the person has been assessed as lacking capacity to consent to sex. This principle is consistent with the Sexual Offences Act (2003), which does not assume a crime has been committed if someone has sex with an adult with learning disabilities. This is unlike the previous Sexual Offences Act (1956), which criminalised all sex involving people considered to be 'severely subnormal'.

Case example: Pamela

Pamela is a 23-year-old woman with Down's syndrome who has been seeing her boyfriend Nigel for about a year. Nigel also has learning disabilities and has known Pamela since their school days. They see each other regularly at college. Pamela lives with her family, who are very supportive of the relationship and often have Nigel in their home. One day Pamela asks her mother if Nigel can stay the night. After the shock of coming to terms with her daughter becoming an adult, Pamela's mother plays for time and says she will think about it. She is not sure how much her daughter understands about sex. How should she respond?

Pamela's mother is not required to follow the Mental Capacity Act (2005) (unless she has been appointed as a deputy for health and welfare decisions by the Court of Protection). Essentially, what happens is a private matter for Pamela's family. Like many mothers facing this situation, Pamela's mother is likely to be concerned about her daughter's understanding of sex, her maturity to manage relationships and the possibility of pregnancy. Pamela may be supported to meet professionals in response to her request for her boyfriend to stay the night – for example, at a family planning clinic, a community nurse or her GP. These professionals need to apply the Mental Capacity Act (2005) when offering support.

The assumption of capacity to consent to sex starts at the age of 16. This is because the Mental Capacity Act (2005) only applies to those over 16. Also, under the Sexual Offences Act (2003), 16 is the age when young people can consent to sex – with people of either the same or opposite sex.

There needs to be a sensible approach to the 'assumption of capacity'. When an individual has a learning disability it is always appropriate to consider and possibly investigate whether they have capacity to consent to sexual relationships. Further, for many individuals with profound learning disabilities, knowledge of their decision-making capacities in other areas of their lives could rule out their potential to consent to any sexual relationships. There may be no need to specifically assess their capacity to consent to sex or to offer sex education. It would be very insensitive, for example, to tell a father of a woman with profound learning disabilities that he should 'assume' his daughter can consent to sexual relationships.

Providing sex education

The second principle of the Mental Capacity Act (2005) challenges services to do what they can to enhance an individual's ability to make decisions themselves. In the context of consent to sexual relationships, this means providing sex education.

Sex education continues to be unevenly available to people with learning disabilities. While some people with learning disabilities may benefit from receiving sex education in school as part of the curriculum, it is unlikely this would be adequate to help people understand and make choices about any sexual relationships as adults. In comparison, other adults may have more opportunities to learn from experience, their friends or family, and media, including the internet.

There is no clear national strategy for providing adults with learning disabilities with sex education. Nor is it clear who is or should be providing the education. The author previously worked in one of a handful of specialist sex education teams for people with learning disabilities, but for the most part these have not survived funding changes. Occasionally, this work is taken up by members of community learning disability teams, for example, psychiatrists, psychologists, nurses or social workers. This generally reflects the individual worker's personal interests rather than being an expectation of their role. Another possibility is that this work may take place within day centres or colleges, but again, the willingness and ability of staff members working in these services to do this cannot be assumed.

Some generic sexual services may be available to people with learning disabilities, for example, counsellors aligned to sexual health clinics or educators in youth centres. It is not necessarily the case that they will understand the context of the sexual lives of people with learning disabilities or that they will have the skills to work with this specific group.

The Resources section at the end of this book identifies both organisations and materials which could help facilitate sex education for individuals. This includes FPA and Image in Action, both of which have been providing training in this specific area for many years (see Resources).

In one notable case, the Court of Protection ruled that a man with learning disabilities was to be provided with sex education under the second principle of the Mental Capacity Act (2005) (D Borough Council v AB [2011] EWHC 101 (COP)). This man was found to lack capacity to consent to sex. Sex education was seen as an opportunity for him to gain capacity and so potentially to be able to make his own decisions in relation to sex. Adults with learning disabilities or their advocates could use this ruling to challenge the unavailability of sex education. The argument to be made to the Court of Protection is a failure of services to comply with this part of the Mental Capacity Act (2005).

'Unwise' sexual relationships

The third principle of the Mental Capacity Act (2005) says that people should not be considered unable to make a decision just because they are considered by others to have made an unwise or bad decision. Services may be tested for their adherence to this principle in relation to the following sexual situations:

- a woman choosing to continue a sexual relationship where there is evidence of abuse by her partner – this could include sexual, physical or financial abuse

- a woman wanting to have a child and not using contraception where there are concerns about her ability to look after a child

- a man having anal sex with another man without using a condom.

The converse of the third principle should be not to ignore issues of capacity just because someone has made what is considered a good decision by other people. Relevant examples here include:

- a woman with learning disabilities agreeing to use contraception

- a man with learning disabilities agreeing to only go out with staff because of the risk of unacceptable sexual behaviour in public

- a woman with learning disabilities agreeing to wait until she gets married before having sex with her boyfriend.

In each of the examples above, given more information and support (principle two), the person with learning disabilities might potentially want to make a different decision that is less acceptable to others. Alternatively, they may be assessed as lacking capacity to make the decision, in which case the requirements for best interest decisions need to be met. This includes the right of the person with learning disabilities (or their advocates) to challenge decisions made about them.

The need to allow people with learning disabilities to make unwise decisions in the area of personal relationships was stressed by Mr Justice Hedley in the Court of Protection:

'In the field of personal relationships that is a very important qualification to the powers of the court. The plain fact is that anyone who has sat in the Family jurisdiction for as long as I have, spends the greater part of their life dealing with the consequences of unwise decisions made in personal relationships. The intention of the Act is not to dress an incapacitous person in forensic cotton wool but to allow them as far as possible to make the same mistakes that all other human beings are at liberty to make and not infrequently do.'
([2013] EWHC 50 (COP))

Assessing capacity under the Mental Capacity Act (2005)

Section 2 and 3 of the Mental Capacity Act (2005) and Chapter 4 of its Code of Practie (2005) set out how capacity to make decisions should be assessed by those working with people with learning disabilities. This covers sexual decisions including consent to sex or a woman's choice to use contraceptives. There are different assessments of capacity to consent to sex undertaken by the courts to determine whether a sexual crime has been committed. These are set out in Chapter 4. Similarly, there are distinct tests for capacity to enter a civil partnership or get married that do not follow to the Mental Capacity Act (2005).

The assessment of capacity under the Mental Capacity Act (2005) is in two stages. The first is assessing whether the person has a mental impairment. This will always be the case if the person is known to have a learning disability. It would also be true if the person has a brain injury, dementia or a mental health condition. Only if a mental impairment is identified can a person's ability to make a specific decision be questioned under the second stage. This requires investigating whether the person is able to:

- understand relevant information about the decision

- retain that information in their mind

- use or weigh that information as part of the decision-making process

- communicate their decision.

Only if they are able to satisfy all four points is the individual assessed as having capacity to make the decision.

Capacity is decision-specific. It cannot be assumed, for example, that a person who lacks capacity to manage their finances lacks capacity to make decisions about sexual relationships. This point was stressed by Mr Justice Hedley in the Court of Protection in a case considering the capacity of a woman with severe learning disabilities to make a decision about continuing a pregnancy:

> 'It is, as I said, very important to bear in mind, particularly in the field of those with significant learning difficulties who may well be unable to function independently in the community in every aspects [sic] of their life, that they may very well retain capacity to make deeply personal decisions about how they conduct their lives. One has in mind the question of choice of partners; the extent to which they wish to be sexually active; the extent to which they may wish to make permanent relationships by way of marriage or indeed civil partnership; the extent to which they may wish to be able to make decisions about their own medical care, including, as in this case, the continuation or termination of a pregnancy. It cannot be the case that merely because a person has significant difficulties in functioning in the community, it can be presumed that they lack capacity to make profoundly personal decisions. They may in fact do so but that has to be assessed on an individual basis.'
> ([2013] EWHC 50 (COP))

There is some subjectivity in the assessment of capacity: one individual may decide that a person with learning disabilities understands enough to make their own decision, while another may take the opposite view. If there is a serious disagreement over the assessment, the expectation is for the Court of Protection to be asked to make the decision.

Court of Protection rulings on capacity to consent to sex

In 2011 the Court of Protection was asked to make a decision on whether a man with learning disabilities had capacity to consent to sex (D Borough Council v AB [2011] EWHC 101 (COP)). This man was known to be having sex with other people with learning disabilities, and had a history of inappropriate and abusive sexual behaviour with members of the public. The services involved had very responsibly made an application to the Court of Protection. This was to ensure both that they were adhering to the law when supporting this man and that his rights were protected.

The court sought expert advice from Dr Ian Hall on what the assessment of capacity to sex should involve. Dr Hall is a psychiatrist working with people with learning disabilities. He suggested that for individuals to have capacity to consent to sex they should understand the following:

■ the mechanics of the act (for example, a penis may go into an anus, vagina or mouth)

■ that only adults over the age of 16 should have sex, and the person needs to be able to distinguish between adults and children

■ that both (or all) parties to the act need to consent to it

■ that there are health risks involved, particularly the acquisition of sexually transmitted diseases (STDs)

■ that sex between a man and a woman may result in the woman becoming pregnant

■ that sex is part of having relationships with people and may have emotional consequences.

Even with this relatively specific list, people could come to different decisions with regard to a person's capacity to consent to sex. For example, what knowledge is required with regard to health risks?

Should it be:

■ knowing you can get sick if you have sex

■ knowing the names of some sexually transmitted diseases

■ knowing how to reduce the risk of sexually transmitted diseases, for example, by limiting partners, avoiding oral sex, vaccination for hepatitis B, using condoms or post-exposure prophylaxis (PEP) for HIV.

Further, in order for someone to have capacity under the Mental Capacity Act (2005), not only must they have knowledge, but they must be able to 'understand, retain, use and weigh up the relevant information'. This suggests that an individual should also have the skills to use strategies to reduce the risk of sexually transmitted diseases, for example, requiring a sexual partner to use a condom, or avoiding unwanted oral sex.

Ideally, people with learning disabilities involved in sexual relationships would have all this knowledge about sexually transmitted diseases as well as the ability to put it into practice. But if this was the standard set in the assessment of capacity very few people with learning disabilities would pass this test, and so may be prevented from having sexual relationships *in their best interests*. This could also undermine an individual's opportunity to develop their skills in asserting themselves in sexual relations through the experience of sexual relationships. It is worth considering how many young adults embark on their sexual lives with limited knowledge and skills but do not look back and regret their early experiences. Nor does society necessarily think they should have been prevented from having those sexual experiences.

Dr Hall's list could be added to. Specifically, it would be good to require people to know that sex should feel good. As was seen in Chapter 1, women with learning disabilities often experience vaginal penetration as painful and do not understand that it can be physically pleasurable. Without this knowledge they are in a poor position to question the quality of their sexual lives or to improve them. This is similarly true of women or men with learning disabilities who endure painful anal sex.

In this case Mr Justice Mostyn in the Court of Protection considered Dr Hall's advice but disagreed with it. He ruled that capacity to consent to sex was 'act-specific'. This means the focus on the mental capacity assessment should be on the sexual activities which an individual may be involved in, and not who they are having sex with. In this way, capacity to consent to sex under the Mental Capacity Act (2005) is very different to that under the Sexual Offences Act (2003), which does consider the person an individual is having sex with, and so is 'person-specific'. Mr Justice Mostyn said that the capacity to consent to sex requires an understanding and awareness:

■ of the mechanics of the act

■ that there are health risks involved, particularly the acquisition of sexually transmitted and sexually transmissible infections

■ that sex between a man and a woman may result in the woman becoming pregnant.

Compared to Dr Hall's sensible and considered recommendations, Mr Justice Mostyn ruled against any requirement for an individual to understand consent in terms of both individuals being adults and wanting to have sex.

Assessed according to Mr Justice Mostyn's criteria, the man was found to lack capacity to consent to sex. The court then ordered the man to be supervised in his best interests to limit his opportunities for having sex. Further, it required the local authority to provide him with sex education, so he could potentially develop the capacity to consent to sex and supervision might no longer be required. The expectation was that his capacity should have been reviewed nine months later.

Although Mr Justice Mostyn suggested that the judgement on capacity to consent to sex could be appealed to a higher court, this has not happened to date. The local authority that made the original application probably achieved the outcome it wanted and so had no reason to appeal: the man being found as lacking capacity to consent to sex, thus enabling the local authority to place restrictions on him in his best interests. For the man himself, or his advocates, appealing could lead to a more demanding test of capacity, which could make it more difficult for him to escape restrictions.

Practical application of Mr Justice Mostyn's ruling

Until a further judgement has been made on the interpretation of capacity to consent to sex under the Mental Capacity Act (2005), services should use Mr Justice Mostyn's assessment. Services will not be adhering to the Mental Capacity Act (2005) if they use a more demanding assessment of an individual's capacity to consent to sex and then make decisions in the person's best interests if they are found to lack capacity.

The only acceptable alternative is to apply to the Court of Protection for a decision on capacity, which may subsequently lead to a new test (potentially closer to Dr Hall's original recommendations and with some view of a person's ability to put knowledge into practice).

The test of capacity is dependent on the genders of the people involved. Table 2.2 sets out what specific information may be required across three possibilities following Mr Justice Mostyn's ruling.

Table 2.2: Information required to determine capacity to consent to sex following Mr Justice Mostyn's ruling

Knowledge required	Two women	Two men	Woman and man
The mechanics of the act	A woman could put her finger or tongue in the other woman's vagina	A man could put his penis in the mouth or anus of the other man	A man's penis could go in the mouth, vagina or anus of the woman.
The health risks involved	People can get sick from having sex	People can get sick from having sex. People can get HIV/AIDS	People can get sick from having sex. People can get HIV/AIDS
That sex between a man and a woman may result in the woman becoming pregnant	A woman can't get pregnant through having sex with a woman	A man can't get pregnant through having sex with a man	A woman can get pregnant if a man puts his penis in the woman's vagina

Line drawings, such as those contained in *Sex and the 3 Rs* (McCarthy & Thomspon, 2016) are extremely useful in helping people with learning disabilities learn about consent to sex and also to assess their capacity.

Case example: Meg

Meg is a woman with Down's syndrome who lives alone in supported accommodation. Staff support her for a few hours each day. She has had a boyfriend, Harry, for a couple of years, and she recently told her keyworker she is 'sleeping' with him. The keyworker contacts the local community team for people with learning disabilities for support. She is concerned that Meg doesn't understand enough about sex and worried about what would happen if she got pregnant. She wonders if it would be in Meg's best interests to try to stop Meg having sex, for example, by saying that her boyfriend can't stay over or even moving her to a group home where staff are available 24 hours a day.

A nurse from the community team spends some time with Meg finding out about her relationship and her understanding of sex. She learns that Meg:

■ Knows that a man puts his penis in the woman's vagina, as this is what her boyfriend does. She says sometimes it hurts a bit but she doesn't mind as she loves him.

- Knows people can get sick from sex. She said she learned about AIDS in college and they were also shown condoms. Her boyfriend Harry doesn't use condoms and she is not worried about this.
- Knows that if a man puts his penis into a woman's vagina, she can get pregnant. However, she did not understand that she could get pregnant having sex with her boyfriend and there was no contraception being used.
- Is not using contraception and doesn't know that women with Down's syndrome may have reduced fertility.
- Prefers it when Harry just sleeps with her and they don't have sex. She says she 'lets him do it' because she thinks that is what girlfriends and boyfriends do. She is worried he would stop being her boyfriend if she 'didn't let him do it'.
- Hasn't had sex with anyone else.
- Knows adults should not have sex with children.

Does Meg have capacity to consent to sex?

Sex for Meg is something she goes along or puts up with. Chapter 1 showed that this is commonly women with learning disabilities' experience of sex with men. While this is far from an ideal mutually pleasurable experience, the question here is whether, under the Mental Capacity Act (2005), Meg has capacity to consent to sex.

The table below compares Meg's knowledge against Mr Justice Mostyn's assessment regarding understanding and awareness in three areas.

Areas of assessment	Meg's knowledge
The mechanics of the act	Meg knows the penis goes in the vagina
There are health risks involved, particularly the acquisition of sexually transmitted and sexually transmissible infections	Meg knows about AIDS and condoms
Sex between a man and a woman may result in the woman becoming pregnant	Meg knows about the possibility of pregnancy

From the above, Meg needs to be assessed as having capacity to consent to sex. This is despite her having significant gaps in her understanding. This includes not relating messages she has received about sexually transmitted diseases and pregnancy to her own sexual relationship. She also lacks the expectation of sexual pleasure for herself or the knowledge that continuing in a relationship without sex should be an option.

Some people may be unhappy about the outcome of this assessment. It is worth noting that Meg would most likely also be found to have capacity to consent to sex using Dr Ian Hall's more demanding assessment. This is because she shows awareness of her agreement to the sex, even if it is not for ideal reasons ('both parties need to consent to the act'). It is also useful to recognise how similar the situation would be for many young women (including those without learning disabilities) in their early sexual encounters with men: where there is limited sexual pleasure, concern about the consequences of saying no and little attention given to the possibilities of sexually transmitted diseases or pregnancy. It may not be ideal consent but using Justice Mostyn's guidance for the Mental Capacity Act (2005) it is good enough.

Because Meg has been found to have capacity to consent to sex on this basis, there are no legal grounds under the Mental Capacity Act (2005) to take action in her best interests that could restrict her opportunities for sex with her boyfriend. Good practice would instead be to offer Meg support to enable her to be more assertive in her relationship, to expect sex to be pleasurable as well as to make informed decisions about the potential of pregnancy and STDs. It would also be ideal if her boyfriend was supported in similar areas, including to pay attention to his partner's experience and desires in a sexual relationship.

In situations like Meg's case example, there can be considerable disagreement about whether an individual has capacity to consent to sex (and whether or what restrictions should be put in place in the person's best interests). The Code of Practice is very clear such disputes should be referred to the Court of Protection. This is an important way of protecting the rights of people with learning disabilities from what might be arbitrary – however well meaning – decision making by services.

Consent to contact with a specific individual

Mr Justice Mostyn ruled that capacity to consent to sex under the Mental Capacity Act (2005) is person-specific. This means it is an assessment of the person independent of whether they are currently having sex or their sexual history – though their description of sexual experiences may help to establish their capacity. It is not the assessment to use when deciding whether a particular sexual event involving a person with learning disabilities was abusive. Instead, the criteria for assessing consent under the Sexual Offences Act (2003) should be tested through the criminal justice system (see Chapter 4).

Having different assessments for consent to sex under the Mental Capacity Act (2005) and the Sexual Offences Act (2003) is inevitable. This is because people who can consent to sex are not immune from being sexually abused. Consent under the Sexual Offences Act (2003) is 'situation and person specific': the ability to consent to sex – or choose not to have sex – is dependent on the situation a person is in. This includes their mental state at the time (for example, had they consumed so much alcohol as to make it impossible to consent?) and whether any inducements or threats were made to convince them to have sex.

If a person with learning disabilities is assessed as being able to consent to sex, the Mental Capacity Act (2005) does allow services to consider restricting contact with individuals where there is a risk of sexual exploitation or abuse. This is because the assessment of a person's capacity to consent to sex is different to an assessment of a person's capacity to have contact with specific individuals with whom they might have sex. This was illustrated in the following case in the Court of Protection.

Derbyshire CC v AC, EC and LC [2014] EWCOP 38

This case involved a woman with severe learning disabilities (presented as having an IQ of 53). During the week she lived with her parents, but at the weekend she stayed with her 'boyfriend'. The woman was reported to have had a history of exploitative and abusive relationships. She had also recently had a child which was taken into care.

The court ruled that she did have capacity to consent to sex but did not have capacity to make decisions regarding her contact with her 'boyfriend'. A key factor which led to this finding was her difficulty in appreciating the implications for her of his convictions for domestic violence. It was also felt she would be unlikely to say no to sex with him because she wanted to be 'lovey dovey'.

Having decided that the woman lacked capacity to make decisions regarding her contact with her boyfriend, the court decided it was in her best interests to deprive her of her liberty by requiring her to live in a residential home. This allowed services to stop any contact with him.

While the outcome of the case is understandable, the route to this decision highlights a problem with the Court of Protection's decisions on capacity to consent to sex under the Mental Capacity Act (2005). It decided that the woman did have capacity to consent to sex, including with this man, even though she could not say no to him.

Best interests decision-making under the Mental Capacity Act (2005)

Only if a person with learning disabilities has been assessed as lacking capacity to consent to sex, or to contact with a specific individual, can best interests decisions, which may or may not restrict their sexual opportunities, be made on their behalf. Before providing guidance, attention will first be given to who can make best interests decisions and the 'excluded decisions' under the Mental Capacity Act (2005).

Who makes best interests decisions?

One of the most remarkable aspects of the Mental Capacity Act (2005) is that it allows multiple people to make best interests decisions on behalf of an individual who has been found unable to make a decision. Section 5.8 of the Code of Practice talks about there being a 'range of decision makers'. For example, if a woman with profound learning disabilities lacks capacity to make decisions about her healthcare:

- her mother could make the decision as to whether to give her over-the-counter painkillers

- her GP could make a best interests decision about medication used to control her epilepsy

- the staff at a respite service could make a best interests decision about how to respond if she has an epileptic fit while staying in their service.

This contrasts with legislation in other countries where decision-making powers are assigned to an individual. For example, in New South Wales, Australia, the woman's mother, as the 'person responsible', would have the legal authority to make all of the decisions above. While the GP could recommend medications, the decision of whether to use them would sit with her mother. Similarly, the respite service would be expected to get the mother's agreement to a plan of care. Only if the mother was appointed as a health and welfare deputy by the Court of Protection would she have this authority in England and Wales.

The NHS, social services and care providers are required to follow the Mental Capacity Act (2005). This means that where an individual with learning disabilities has been assessed as lacking capacity to make a specific decision, services need to make best interests decisions in line with the Code of Practice. This may apply in the following examples:

- A care provider deciding whether to supervise a person with learning disabilities in their best interests to prevent the individual having contact with a man who may sexually abuse them.

- Social services deciding whether it is in the best interests of a man with learning disabilities to stop attending a day service because of the risk of him sexually abusing the other people who use the service.

- Social services deciding if it is in the best interests of a person with learning disabilities to move them to another residential service because of the risk of unconsented sex with another resident.

- A care provider deciding if it is in the best interests of a person with learning disabilities not to allow a visitor to spend time alone with them because of concerns about sexual contact.

- An NHS doctor deciding if it is the best interests of a woman with learning disabilities to use contraception when she lacks capacity to consent to sex and make decisions about contraception.

As will be seen below, for many of these decisions authority is required from the Court of Protection.

Understanding the 'excluded decisions': consent to sexual relationships

The Mental Capacity Act (2005) sets out a number of 'excluded decisions' which cannot be made by anyone in a person's best interests. These include:

- consent to sexual relationships

- consent to entering into or ending a civil partnership or marriage

- consent to adoption of a person's child.

This means that no one can give legally valid consent on behalf of a person with learning disabilities who lacks capacity to make these decisions themselves. If a person with learning disabilities has been assessed as lacking capacity to consent to sex, a service cannot decide that it is in the person's best interests to have sex. However, it may not be in the person's best interests for a service to ensure that they don't have sex. Sometimes it will be in a person's best interests for supervision to stop short of preventing sexual opportunities. This is suggested by the following case in the Court of Protection involving a woman and man with severe learning disabilities who had a sexual relationship where the man was initially assessed as lacking capacity to consent to sex.

NHS Trust v DE [2013] EWCH 2562

The focus of this case was on determining the best interests of a man with learning disabilities in a relationship with a woman with learning disabilities. The couple had previously had a child which was taken into care. At the time of the hearing, the couple were being kept apart from each other to prevent any sexual contact between them. This separation was causing them both distress. The court considered and agreed that it was in the man's best interests to be sterilised and then for the couple to resume contact in his/their best interests. In making the decision, attention was given to the fifth principle of the Mental Capacity Act (2005):

Before the act is done, or the decision is made, regard must be had to whether the purpose for which it is needed can be as effectively achieved in a way that is less restrictive of the person's rights and freedom of action.

This is why this guide has interpreted this principle as:

Where a person with learning disabilities lacks capacity to consent to sex, it is not always in their best interests to stop them having sex.

This judgement should inform other best interests decisions where an individual with learning disabilities is known to have sex, or where there is a possibility of sex with another person – whether or not the other person has capacity to consent to sex. In some situations it may be in the person's best interests to restrict sexual opportunities, whereas in others it may not.

Factors that could inform this decision would include:

■ how mutual the relationship is likely to be – both sexually and otherwise

■ the difference in the abilities of those involved

■ the possibility of pregnancy in opposite-sex relationships

■ the risks of STDs and whether these can be mitigated, for example, by hepatitis B vaccination

■ the potential of adverse responses from others, for example, if a family member may remove their relative from the service if any sexual contact is not prevented.

This judgement was also significant because of the best interests decision to sterilise the man. See Chapter 3 on contraception and sterilisation for further discussion of these issues.

Case example: not always stopping sex when capacity to consent is lacking

Two male clients are found together by a staff member in one of their bedrooms. One of them is visiting the other's group home because it is someone else in the home's birthday.

Just one man has his trousers and pants down exposing a flaccid penis. The other man has his hand on this penis. The contact stops as soon as the staff member sees them and both men look anxious.

The staff member knows the men to be good friends. Both have limited verbal skills and are always supported by staff when they are outside either their homes or their shared day centre.

How might the staff member respond?

The staff member should make a quick judgement as to whether they have interrupted a private moment between the two men, or walked in on an act of sexual abuse. They may want to apologise for not having permission to go into the bedroom.

If, as it appears, there are no serious concerns about one man sexually abusing the other, it could be appropriate to suggest that the men leave the room to join the party. As much as possible, the staff member may want to avoid the men thinking that they have done something wrong.

It could be appropriate to raise a safeguarding alert for the men. This would hopefully lead to a sensitive investigation of both men's understanding of and consent to what was happening.

What do the men need to understand in order to have capacity to consent to this sexual contact?

Mr Justice Mostyn's capacity assessment is relevant here. This says that the men would need to understand the 'mechanics of the act' and that there are health risks involved. There would be no requirement for them to have knowledge about conception.

The need for the men to understand the health risks of sex may find one or both of them lacking capacity to consent to sex. This could be considered an unfair demand if neither of them have a sexually transmitted disease and there is no evidence of them having sex with anyone else.

Should the men be prevented from spending time alone together if one or both of them lack capacity to consent to sex, but there is no evidence of abuse?

A best interests decision needs to be made regarding the possibility of the men spending time alone together. Noting principle five of the Mental Capacity Act (2005), which requires a consideration of what decision may be least restrictive, it is not necessarily in the men's best interests to be supervised to such an extent that there is no opportunity for them to be alone. The judgement of NHS Trust v DE [2013] EWHC 2562 (see p33) noted how distressing restrictions on a relationship was for a man with learning disabilities. Even if sex education fails to skill the men with capacity to consent to sex it may not be in their best interest to ensure there is no further opportunity for further sexual contact between them.

There may be other factors to consider, for example, if a parent of one of the men said they would withdraw their son from the day centre if there was further sexual contact and so effectively end their relationship.

Facilitating sexual opportunities for people unable to consent to sex

At times in learning disability services, the suggestion is made that a person is 'sexually frustrated' and may benefit from accessing a prostitute to 'relieve' their sexual tension. Consistently, the person is a man with learning disabilities and the suggestion is for a female prostitute. Any underlying stereotypical assumptions of men needing sex, women servicing men and heterosexuality should first be challenged before assessing the person's capacity to consent to sex.

If the person is found to lack capacity to consent to sex, the Mental Capacity Act (2005) does not support services facilitating access to prostitutes. This is because to do so could be seen as making a best interests decision for them to have sex: an excluded decision – the distinction being between 'facilitating' rather than 'not stopping'. However, an argument about best interests could be made if someone was instead being enlisted to help the person (again, probably a man) learn how to masturbate.

Where a person with learning disabilities is assessed as having capacity to consent to sex, services still need to be extremely cautious about providing any support to access prostitutes – whether this be giving information about local brothels, driving the person to one or being involved in the financial transaction. This is because many aspects of prostitution, including curb crawling and pimping, remain illegal in the UK. Further, many women working as prostitutes are sexually and financially exploited by their pimps.

Restricting sexual opportunities in an individual's best interests

It will generally be in the best interests of a person with learning disabilities to restrict sexual opportunities to prevent them from either being sexual abused or sexually abusing. However, at times it may not be. For example, it may or may not be in an individual's best interests to:

- limit contact with someone who may sexually abuse them, for example, not allowing a potential abuser into the residential service where the person with learning disabilities lives

- increase supervision when out to reduce the risk of a man with learning disabilities sexually abusing children or adults in the general public

- increase supervision when out to reduce the risk of the person being sexually exploited

- move a person away from a service where they may be at risk of being sexually abused or sexually abusing others

■ place restrictions on the life of a man with learning disabilities who frequently exposes himself when out (regardless of whether this is intentional).

Very often these decisions require the person to have access to the safeguards in the Mental Capacity Act (2005), of the Court of Protection or Deprivation of Liberty Safeguards. These safeguards are there to ensure that any decisions made are lawful, apply only to individuals who lack capacity to make a decision themselves and represent their best interests.

Services often see calls to access these safeguards as a challenge to the decisions they are making. While at times this might be the case, even if decisions are not disputed, the law often requires best interests decisions to be validated by these safeguards.

A positive obligation to ensure people with learning disabilities' rights are protected

Under the European Convention on Human Rights there is a 'positive obligation' on states to ensure individual rights are protected. This means, for example, that it is unacceptable for local authorities to make best interests decisions for individuals without making sure they have access to the safeguards required in law. It is not enough for local authorities to respond only when challenged about a best interests decision – whether this be by the person, a family member or another advocate. This has been emphasised in a number of UK court judgements.

One of the most notable examples was the case of Steven Neary, a man with learning disabilities, for whom Hillingdon local authority made the decision not to allow him to return to live with his father after an agreed stay in a respite service (LB Hillingdon v Steven Neary [2011] EWHC 1377). The local authority was severely criticised for:

■ the unacceptable quality of its best interests decision for Steven Neary not to return home

■ unlawfully depriving Steven Neary of his liberty

■ failing to ensure timely access to an independent mental capacity advocate

■ the delay in bringing the matter to the Court of Protection.

The judge's comments highlight the responsibility of local authorities to be proactive in accessing the Court of Protection:

'I have already indicated that the protracted delay in applying to court in this case was highly unfortunate. There are repeated references, particularly by the service manager, to the burden being on Mr Neary to take the matter to court if he wished to challenge what was happening. That approach cannot be right. I have already referred to the decision in Re S, which rightly observes that the practical and evidential burden is on a local authority to demonstrate that its arrangements are better than those that can be achieved within the family. It will discharge the practical burden by ensuring that there is a proper forum for decision. It will not do so by allowing the situation it has brought about to continue by default. Nor is it an answer to say, as Hillingdon has done, that Mr Neary could always have gone to court himself, and that it had told him so. It was Steven's rights, and not those of his father, that were in issue. Moreover, local authorities have the advantage over individuals both in terms of experience and, even nowadays, depth of pocket. The fact that an individual does not bring a matter to court does not relieve the local authority of the obligation to act, it redoubles it.'
(para. 196, LB Hillingdon v Steven Neary [2011] EWHC 1377)

A more recent case (Somerset v MK [2014] EWCOP B25, [2014] MHLO 146) has many parallels with the Steven Neary case. Here a woman with learning disabilities was prevented from returning to her family home by the local authority because of a concern about potential abuse by her mother. While the local authority may have been well meaning, it lacked the authority to take this action without the authority of the court, which it had not sought. The local authority was also heavily criticised for its lack of knowledge of the Mental Capacity Act (2005).

These cases emphasise the need to ensure the safeguards under the Mental Capacity Act (2005) are made available, and where necessary, legal authority sought from court. This includes cases where a best interests decision is made to put restrictions on a person with learning disabilities which may either reduce the risk of them being sexually abused or sexually abusing others.

Sir James Munby set out the very limited powers of local authorities to enforce decisions concerning people with learning disabilities without the authority of the court:

'What emerges from this is that, whatever the extent of a local authority's positive obligations under Article 5, its duties, and more important its powers, are limited. In essence, its duties are threefold: a duty in appropriate circumstances to investigate; a duty in appropriate circumstances to provide supporting services; and a duty in appropriate circumstances to refer the matter to the court. But, and this is a key message, whatever the positive obligations of

a local authority under Article 5 may be, they do not clothe it with any power to regulate, control, compel, restrain, confine or coerce. A local authority which seeks to do so must either point to specific statutory authority for what it is doing – and, as I have pointed out, such statutory powers are, by and large, lacking in cases such as this – or obtain the appropriate sanction of the court. Of course if there is immediate threat to life or limb a local authority will be justified in taking protective (including compulsory) steps ... but it must follow up any such intervention with an immediate application to the court.'
(Re A (Adult) and Re C (Child); A Local Authority v A [2010] EWHC 978 (Fam))

Which safeguards apply when considering restricting sexual opportunities?

The safeguards which should be used depend on where the person is living, for example:

- If they are living in a care home or hospital – or if it is proposed to move the person to a care home or hospital – the Deprivation of Liberty Safeguards may be used. However, it may still be necessary to make an application to the Court of Protection (see below).

- If they are living in other accommodation supported by staff the Court of Protection should be used.

- If they are living with family the Court of Protection may be used.

Case law has suggested that there is a higher threshold for what restrictions a family can place on a person with learning disabilities compared to funded services without needing the authority of the Court of Protection for these restrictions. A key case is Re A (Adult) and (Re C (Child); A Local Authority v A [2010] EWHC 978 (Fam) and its subsequent appeal, Re P and Q; P and Q v Surrey County Council; sub nom Re MIG and MEG [2011] EWCA Civ 190). Here an adult woman with learning disabilities was locked in her bedroom during the night for her and other family members' safety. The court ruled that she was not being deprived of her liberty and there was no authority for the state (including social services) to direct the family on how to support her. The court did, however, confirm that social services should investigate concerns about people with learning disabilities living in the family home, and may at times seek the authority from the Court of Protection if they believe changes in support arrangements are needed.

If it was decided that a person with learning disabilities should be locked in their bedroom in a funded service overnight, authorisation would need to be sought through either the Deprivation of Liberty Safeguards or the Court of Protection.

Such a restriction would be unlikely to be supported as being in the person's best interests. For example, having an alert alarm on the bedroom door and waking staff is likely to be a safer and less restrictive alternative.

Deprivation of Liberty Safeguards

The expression 'deprivation of liberty' is a legal term taken from the European Convention on Human Rights and incorporated into UK law. Essentially, a person requires legal safeguards if they are deprived of their liberty. This includes cases where the aim of restrictions is to protect the individual from being sexually abused or to prevent them from sexually abusing others.

The Deprivation of Liberty Safeguards are a relatively new way to legally place restrictions on an individual's freedom. Other legal systems which allow this are the Mental Health Act (1983), and the criminal justice system. The Deprivation of Liberty Safeguards only support restrictions if:

■ the person is 18 or over

■ the person has been assessed as lacking capacity to make decisions about the risks they are exposing themselves or other people to

■ the restrictions imposed satisfy the requirements of being in the person's best interests.

These requirements are checked by 'assessors' when an application is made to the local authority for a 'standard authorisation'. If all requirements are met, the deprivation of the person's liberty is 'authorised'.

When applications for standard authorisations need to be made

Only if a person with learning disabilities is living in a care home or hospital can legal safeguards be available through the Deprivation of Liberty Safeguards. For example, a care home or hospital should make an application for a 'standard authorisation' to the local authority if they are, or are proposing:

■ requiring a person with learning disabilities to be accompanied by staff when out to reduce the risk of them being sexually abused

■ requiring a person with learning disabilities to be accompanied by staff when out to reduce the risk of them sexually abusing others (including exposing themselves – regardless of whether or not this is intentional).

If these restrictions are already occurring, an urgent authorisation needs to be put in place while the application for a standard authorisation is considered by assessors.

In other settings, authority to deprive a person of their liberty needs to come directly from the Court of Protection. For example, if a day or supported living service wished to constantly supervise a person when out in the community because of the risk of them being sexually exploited, an application should be made to the Court of Protection by the service or the funder of this service.

Moving a person

If it is proposed to move a person in their best interests to a care home or hospital to reduce the risk of them being sexually abused or sexually abusing, an application for a standard authorisation needs to be made by the new service. If the person has already moved for these reasons, an urgent authorisation needs to be put in place by the new care home or hospital while the assessors for the standard authorisation confirm (or otherwise) that the move is in the person's best interests.

Important additional safeguards incorporated into the Deprivation of Liberty Safeguards are the right of access to an independent mental capacity advocate (IMCA) and the right of the person, or any personal representative or IMCA, to have decisions reviewed by the Court of Protection. One judgement from a previous case (Neary; see p37) is that local authorities need to be proactive in taking disputes about whether restrictions are in a person's best interests to the Court of Protection, rather than potentially taking advantage of any difficulties the person or their representatives might have in raising a challenge in the Court of Protection.

Restricting contact with a potential sexual abuser

Sometimes there is a concern about a person with learning disabilities living in a care home or hospital being sexually abused by a visitor – either within or away from the service. This might be a family member, a previous staff member or another person with learning disabilities. Appropriate routes to address any such concerns are through the police and adult safeguarding procedures.

It may be proposed to restrict contact with the alleged abuser in the best interests of the person with learning disabilities. This could be by requiring supervised visits or not allowing the alleged abuser into the service. Authority for such restrictions needs to come directly from the Court of Protection. Department of Health guidance has advised that the Deprivation of Liberty Safeguards should not be used to restrict contact with a named potential abuser other than as a short-term measure (Department of Health, 2010).

Deprivation of liberty key points

■ Action taken in the best interests of an individual may be a deprivation of their liberty under Article 5 of the European Convention on Human Rights. This includes steps taken to reduce the risk of the person being sexually abused or sexually abusing others.

■ Authority for restrictions should be sought from the Court of Protection prior to putting these in place, unless there is an imminent risk to life or limb.

■ If the individual lives in a care home or hospital, the Deprivation of Liberty Safeguards may be used to require supervision when the person is out.

■ Where the Deprivation of Liberty Safeguards are used, local authorities should still apply to the Court of Protection to ensure any restrictions are lawful.

Case example: different authority for different settings

Mike is a 42-year-old man with learning disabilities who often walks alone around his local area and is known to a lot of people in the local community. There was a recent incident where it is alleged he tried to touch the bottom of a seven-year-old girl when he went alone to a local park. The family of the girl know Mike and didn't want the police involved.

Regardless of where Mike is living, the local authority should ensure the safeguarding processes for both adults and children are followed.

In a family home

If Mike is living in the family home, his parents could make the decision for him not to go out alone for a period. They do not require any external authority to make this decision, which could be appropriate in the circumstances. Family members have no obligation to adhere to the Mental Health Act (2005) (unless they hold the formal powers of a deputy or attorney). Therefore, they do not need to undertake capacity assessments or follow the guidance for making best interests decisions.

If the local authority was concerned about the family's decision, they would need to make an application to the Court of Protection to challenge it. Potentially this could be appropriate if, for example, to prevent Mike going out alone he was regularly locked in his bedroom with no access to the toilet while his parents were out. As noted in Sir James Munby's comments above, the threshold for taking action without the prior authority of the court is 'immediate threat to life or limb' (Re A (Adult) and Re C (Child); A Local Authority v A [2010] EWHC 978 (Fam)).

In a care home (or hospital)

If Mike is living in a care home, there is a requirement for those providing his care to follow the Mental Capacity Act (2005). Mike should be assessed as to whether he has capacity to decide if he should or should not go out unaccompanied. To have capacity, he would need to recognise the risk to him of a criminal prosecution for a similar allegation of sexual assault, as well as have some understanding of the experience of the child. If he was assessed as having capacity to make this decision, there would be no authority to insist he only went out with staff.

If Mike was assessed as lacking capacity to make this decision, it may in his best interests to ensure he is supervised at all times when out for a period. To implement such a regime, the care home would need to make an application for a standard authorisation and put in place an urgent authorisation (so that it could start the supervision while awaiting the outcome of the assessments for the standard authorisation).

If a standard authorisation is granted supporting supervision at all times when out, it may still be necessary for the care provider or local authority to make an application to the Court of Protection to ensure the restrictions are legal. This would be the case if:

- it was unclear or disputed whether Mike had capacity to make a decision about going out alone
- Mike was unwilling to comply with the restrictions, for example, he tried going out by himself when staff weren't watching him
- there was a disagreement about whether the restrictions were in his best interests – this could be between professionals and/or family members.

Even if none of the above apply, an early application to the Court of Protection may still need to be made, particularly if the restrictions are to be ongoing. This is because, however well meaning, the restrictions represent a serious infringement on Mike's liberty under Article 5 of the European Convention on Human Rights. As such, he is 'entitled to take proceedings by which the lawfulness of his detention shall be decided speedily by a court'. From the finding of the Steven Neary case quoted previously, it is clear that the responsibility is on the local authority to take the matter to court, regardless of the desire or ability of Mike or any of his representatives to do so.

In supported living

If Mike was living in a supported living service, a mental capacity assessment would also need to be undertaken regarding his ability to make a decision about going out by himself. If he was found to lack capacity to make this decision, and it was proposed that he should only be allowed out when accompanied by staff, authority for this would need to come directly from the Court of Protection. In such a case, an urgent application to the court is recommended (see SCIE (2011) good practice guidance in accessing the Court of Protection). It would be very difficult to argue that there was an immediate risk to life or limb for Mike that permitted such restrictions being put in place prior to a court hearing.

In some supported living services, it could be impractical to ensure staff supervision at all times, for example, if Mike only receives a few hours of support in his home each week. In such a case it might be suggested that Mike should move somewhere where this is achievable – even for a temporary period. Again, such a move and the proposed restrictions should not be actioned without the prior authority of the Court of Protection.

When to make applications to the Court of Protection

Applications should be made to the Court of Protection if is proposed to take any of the following actions in the best interests of a person with learning disabilities:

- Imposing restrictions on their freedom of movement to reduce the risk of sexual abuse, regardless of whether the person with learning disabilities is a potential perpetrator or victim.
- Removing someone against their wishes, or the wishes of family members, from their residence, where they may be at risk of being sexually abused or sexually abusing.
- To restrict contact with specific individuals who may sexually abuse them.

Local authorities have been strongly criticised, and sometimes fined, for delays in bringing such matters in front of the courts. Action in a person's best interests may only take place prior to court authority if there is an imminent danger to life or limb.

Case example: potential sexual exploitation

Sarah, a woman with learning disabilities, lives in her own flat. She receives six hours support a week to help her with budgeting, cooking and cleaning. The support worker learns that a man often stays in her flat. The support worker has not met this man, but one time they arrived and heard a man tell Sarah not to let them in. Sarah afterwards explained that this was her boyfriend Ahmad – she doesn't know his surname. Sarah says that she and Ahmad have sex and that they will be getting married. She does not know where he lives but does have his mobile phone number. Sarah is 55 and is not known to be using contraception.

Consider the following:

- Should this be a safeguarding referral to the local authority?
- What is it reasonable for Sarah's service to ask her about this relationship?
- What would you want Sarah to understand in order for her to have capacity to consent to having sex with this man?

1. Should this be a safeguarding referral to the local authority?

There are a few flags which raise concerns about potential abuse or exploitation:

■ Sarah has learning disabilities.

■ The man is avoiding contact with others.

■ Sarah does not know the man's full name or where he lives.

The staff member should discuss their concerns with both Sarah and senior staff members in their organisation. This may help establish one of the following three responses:

1. Sarah has capacity to make choices about this relationship and whether the local authority should be involved (including if the relationship is exploitative or abusive). Her wishes regarding whether or not this case should be referred to the local authority may need to be respected.

2. Sarah does not have capacity to make choices about this relationship due to a likely power imbalance. A referral to the local authority should be made.

3. The status of the relationship and Sarah's ability to make decisions about it are unclear. If Sarah agrees to a referral to the local authority, this should happen. If she objects, the organisation needs to clearly identify the grounds for either making or not making a referral to the local authority.

The third response may be guided by many factors, including:

■ the ability of and opportunity for the organisation to clarify what might be happening and to assess Sarah's capacity to make related decisions

■ the ability of and opportunity for the organisation to provide ongoing support for what could be an abusive relationship

■ Sarah's willingness to discuss the relationship

■ the man's willingness to identify himself and to meet with staff

■ whether Sarah's relationship history includes exploitation

■ evidence of other potential abuse, for example, financial

■ any signs of planning for a marriage, especially if it may take place overseas.

Only if the organisation is confident that abuse or exploitation is not occurring, or if it is well placed to provide Sarah with ongoing support, is it justifiable not to make a referral to the local authority. In most cases a referral should be made and the reasons for doing so against Sarah's wishes should ideally be explained to her.

2. What is it reasonable for Sarah's service to ask her about this relationship?

The service is there to provide support with 'budgeting, cooking and cleaning'. This raises the question as to whether it is appropriate for the support worker or other staff members in their organisation to explore Sarah's relationship with her and potentially ask her intimate questions, including questions about sex. While it could be desirable to have a specialist worker to cover this ground, in practice they may not be available locally. Further, there would be similar issues of potentially going against Sarah's wishes for privacy and confidentiality by involving an external professional, as for the decision of whether to make a referral to the local authority.

As part of holistic support, it is not unreasonable for a support worker or another staff member in the service to ask Sarah questions about the relationship. She will always have the option to decline discussing it, but may potentially value the opportunity to talk.

3. What would you want Sarah to understand in order for her to have capacity to consent to having sex with this man?

Following the guidance issued by Mr Justice Mostyn, Sarah would have capacity to consent to sex with this man (or any other) under the Mental Capacity Act (2005) if she can understand (retain and weigh up) the following:

- the mechanics of the act
- the fact that there are health risks involved, particularly the risk of sexually transmitted diseases
- the fact that sex between a man and a woman may result in the woman becoming pregnant.

Because of her age, Sarah may also need to understand how extremely unlikely it would be for her to get pregnant due to the menopause. For example, her capacity to consent to sex would be questionable if she believed she was going to have a child with the man.

Young people between the ages of 16 and 18

In general, the Mental Capacity Act (2005) applies to all people aged 16 and over. Also, the age of consent for sex (regardless of gender) is 16. However, there are some differences in how young people between the ages of 16 and 18 should be supported if they are involved in a sexual relationship.

These differences apply if the young person has been assessed as lacking capacity to make decisions about sex under the Mental Capacity Act (2005). The capacity assessment discussed above still applies.

Parental responsibility

Parental responsibility for young people continues up to the age of 18. Therefore, services making decisions about how to support a young person assessed as lacking capacity to make decisions about sex need those with parental responsibility to support their proposals. This includes cases where the young person is living temporarily (for example, at a residential school) or permanently away from their parent(s).

Those with parental responsibility for young people are not required to follow the Mental Capacity Act Code of Practice (2005) in making their decisions; the only exception being if they have been appointed as a personal welfare deputy by the Court of Protection. Parental responsibility can only be overridden by a legal process. Generally, this would be through the Family Court. It would need to be shown that the parent's decision was putting the young person at significant risk of neglect or abuse. This is best illustrated by an example, such as the one below.

Case example: Rita

Rita is a 17-year-old woman with learning disabilities. She has a very strong desire to have a boyfriend and get married. She will often approach men asking them to be her boyfriend and there is a fear that she will be sexually exploited. The residential college she attends has assessed Rita as lacking capacity to consent to sex. The college believes it is in Rita's best interests not to be allowed out of the college by herself. However, Rita's mother disagrees with this plan. While she shares the concern about the risk of sexual exploitation, she believes the plan is unnecessarily restrictive and takes away Rita's opportunity to learn from experience. She also explains that Rita would often go out by herself when at home.

Without the authority of Rita's mother, the college cannot restrict her movements as they had intended. The college could apply to the Family Court if it believed that the mother's decision was putting Rita at serious risk.

If Rita was 18, the college would not need her mother's authority, as parental responsibility would no longer apply. However, there would be both a serious dispute about Rita's best interests and, potentially, the college's restrictions could amount to a deprivation of her liberty. The college should apply to the Court of Protection for a decision on Rita's best interests and authority for the proposed restrictions.

Over the age of 18, under the Mental Capacity Act (2005) services are expected to consult with parents but are able to make best interest decisions which do not reflect their views (though this dispute about what is in an adult's best interests may need to be referred to the Court of Protection).

Deprivation of Liberty Safeguards and under 18s

The deprivation of liberty safeguards do not apply to people under the age of 18. Services working with young people should always apply to the Court of Protection or Family Court if the restrictions implemented in the best interests of a young person may amount to a deprivation of their liberty. This is regardless of the agreement of those with parental responsibility. This could include the following situations:

■ Continuously supervising a young man with learning disabilities living in a care home to reduce the risk of him exposing himself or touching people in the community.

■ Making a young woman with learning disabilities wear clothing which restricts her access to her genitals to prevent her causing injury to herself because of frequent attempts to masturbate.

■ Stopping a young man with learning disabilities from going out unaccompanied from a residential college because he is known to seek sex with men and there is a concern that he may be sexually exploited or at risk of HIV infection.

Chapter 3: Decisions concerning contraception, sterilisation and pregnancy under the Mental Capacity Act (2005)

The growing acceptance of people with learning disabilities having sex and relationships is not matched by support for people with learning disabilities to have children. Parents with learning disabilities remain rare. In part, this is because some syndromes – including Down's, Turner and Prader-Willi syndromes – are associated with reduced fertility or infertility. Also, services and families often do what they can to make sure that people with learning disabilities do not become parents – whether this be restricting sexual opportunities or facilitating contraception. This is not the place to discuss the ethical issues that arise here. Instead, the focus is on ensuring the relevant decisions comply with the Mental Capacity Act (2005).

In the preceding chapter, information was given about when it may be possible to restrict people's sexual opportunities in their best interests and the legal safeguards they should be afforded if this is proposed. This chapter addresses decisions about contraception after first looking at the legal requirements surrounding sterilisation.

Sterilisation

Sterilisation is a medical intervention that has a special status in law. Decisions about 'non-therapeutic' sterilisations cannot be made in a person's best interests without the authority of the courts. This is set out in the Mental Capacity Act

Code of Practice (2005) and Practice Direction E (applications related to serious medical treatment for Part 9 of the Court of Protection Rules (2007)).

Non-therapeutic sterilisations are those where the aim is to prevent either a woman or man having children. Therapeutic sterilisations are when the aim of the procedure is for a health benefit but an indirect consequence is the loss of the potential to have children. For example, hysterectomies are often carried out because of ovarian, uterine or cervical cancers, and leave the woman sterile. In these cases, it would be possible for a hysterectomy to be performed in the best interests of a woman with learning disabilities without reference to the Court of Protection.

Hysterectomies are sometimes carried out in cases where women experience heavy/painful periods. If this is proposed in the best interests of a woman with learning disabilities, the decision should be referred to the Court of Protection. This is because a hysterectomy in these circumstances is unlikely to satisfy principle 5 of the Mental Capacity Act (2005), which requires consideration of less restrictive alternatives. Relevant here is a judgement by the Court of Appeal, which ruled that insertion of a hormone-releasing intrauterine system was preferable to sterilisation or a hysterectomy for a woman with severe learning disabilities with heavy periods, as it was less invasive (SL v SL [2000] EWCA Civ 162).

There are more recent cases where the courts have been asked to decide whether sterilisation is in the best interests of a person with learning disabilities.

Sterilisation of a man with learning disabilities (NHS Trust v DE [2013] EWHC 2562)

This unusual case (also discussed in Chapter 2) concerned the potential sterilisation of a man with learning disabilities who was in a long-term relationship with a woman with learning disabilities. The couple had previously had a child which was taken into care. In response to this, the couple were supervised to an extent that took away any opportunity for them to have sex. This surveillance put great pressure on their relationship.

The man was initially found to be lacking capacity to consent to sex but after extensive education was reassessed as gaining capacity. He did not have capacity to make a decision about having a vasectomy. The court ruled that sterilisation was in the man's best interests, as it offered him a less restrictive regime than the supervision which had been imposed on his relationship.

Sex, Personal Relationships and the Law for Adults with Learning Disabilities
© Pavilion Publishing and Media Ltd and its licensors 2018.

Sterilisation and women with learning disabilities: [2013] EWHC 242 (COP) and [2015] EWCOP 4

Mr Justice Cobb ruled in favour of and against sterilisation in two cases involving women with learning disabilities. The first of these involved a woman with severe learning disabilities whose parents proposed sterilisation ([2013] EWHC 242 (COP)). They were concerned about her growing interest in the opposite sex and vulnerability to sexual exploitation. The judge disagreed with either contraception or sterilisation being in her best interests, as the woman was well supervised and showed no desire to have a sexual relationship.

In the second case Mr Justice Cobb did agree that sterilisation was in the best interests of a woman with learning disabilities (identified as DD) ([2015] EWCOP 4). At the time of the hearing, she was in a long-term sexual relationship with a man with learning disabilities. The woman had previously had six children which had all been taken into care. Despite this, she was motivated to have further children and had previously concealed pregnancies to avoid state intrusion in her life. The court accepted evidence suggesting the woman's life was at risk if she had another pregnancy. The court specified that in order to be assessed as having capacity to make her own decisions regarding contraception and sterilisation, the woman would have to understand these risks:

'i) the risk of a thrombo-embolic disease during any future pregnancy (as mentioned above, DD suffered a thrombotic embolism during her fourth pregnancy);

ii) the risk of delivering a pre-term infant (her fourth child was born at 29 weeks and suffered breathing difficulties);

iii) the impact on DD's mental and emotional health of any further pregnancy (DD has suffered from a delusional disorder following her second and third pregnancies);

iv) the additional risks of a home birth for DD (which would always be likely to be her preferred mode of delivery);

v) the risk of placenta accreta; as mentioned above ([9](ii)), given that DD has undergone four caesarean sections, this would be particularly dangerous for DD, given the significant risk of extensive haemorrhaging at the point of removal; if bleeding cannot be stemmed DD faces the prospect of hysterectomy;

vi) that she faces considerable (and, with each pregnancy, increasing) risks to her life through the delivery of any child. Vaginal birth after caesarean carries considerable risks associated with rupture of the uterus; this is particularly acute given that the uterine wall is now seen to be 'tissue thin'; caesarean section carries risk of operative failure, adhesions or bowel or bladder injury, and the general risks associated with general anaesthetic.'
([2015] EWCOP 4)

DD was found to lack capacity, and a laparoscopicsterilisation (obstruction of the fallopian tubes by keyhole surgery) was ruled to be in her best interests. To implement this judgement, authority was given to force entry into the woman's home and to use 'necessary restraint'.

The above cases suggest that sterilisation will not be supported by the courts in a person's best interests if there is no evidence of, or desire for, sexual activity. (See also Re A (Male Sterilisation) [2000] 1 FLR 549, where sterilisation of a man with Down's syndrome 'just in case' was rejected.) The courts will always look at the possibility of contraception as an alternative to sterilisation, because it may be less invasive and reversible. See also Rowlands and Amy (2018).

Contraception

The sensitivity and safeguards regarding sterilising people with learning disabilities are not matched when it comes to decisions about contraception. These are essentially decisions concerning women with learning disabilities. There are two reasons for this. First, contraception is often seen as a woman's responsibility, Second, condoms are the only contraception option for men who have penetrative sex with women.

In the case described earlier where a vasectomy was approved (NHS Trust v DE [2013] EWCH 2562), condom use was considered. The judge found condoms to be an unsatisfactory option because of the high risk of pregnancy, exacerbated by concerns about the man's technique and how consistently he would use them. My own work with men with a range of abilities supports the judge's pessimism of condoms being a reliable alternative to sterilisation if the goal is to avoid pregnancy.

Michelle McCarthy undertook research into women with learning disabilities' use of contraception (2010). Women with learning disabilities, carers and doctors were interviewed about how decisions about the women's use of contraception were made. Rarely were women with learning disabilities found to be making their own decisions about using contraction. Typically, the women had been accompanied to see a doctor by a family member or paid carer who was keen to avoid any risk of pregnancy.

The doctors generally paid little attention to the women with learning disabilities' views about having children, conceding to the wishes of those who accompanied the women. Further, the decision about which form of contraception was prescribed showed little concern for the women with learning disabilities having control over their fertility – including having the choice not to use contraception. This was evident from the use of long-acting injectable contraceptives in about half of the cases, a rate much higher than other women's use in the UK. When oral contraception was prescribed, the doctors said they relied on the people accompanying the women to ensure the pill was taken.

This research was conducted before the implementation of the Mental Capacity Act (2005), but is likely to reflect the current decision-making process for many women with learning disabilities using contraception – not least because many women will have been prescribed contraception before this legislation was implemented in 2007, and their use of it may not have been reviewed since.

The Mental Capacity Act (2005) requires a different decision-making process. Using or not using contraception, and the type of contraception, should be choices made by women with learning disabilities. Potentially 'unwise choices' – for example, wanting a baby which is likely to be taken into care – need to be accepted. Only if a woman has been found to lack capacity to make a decision about contraception can a best interests decision to prescribe it be made.

Long-term use of contraception can be as effective as sterilisation in ensuring women do not get pregnant and have children. However, the Mental Capacity Act (2005) does not give women with learning disabilities who are prescribed contraception equivalent safeguards to those available for sterilisation. This is of concern, not least because Michelle McCarthy's work shows us that we need to be concerned about how decisions about contraception are made in practice.

Capacity to make a decision about contraception

The courts have given guidance on how capacity to make decisions about contraceptives should be assessed (A Local Authority v A [2010] EWHC 1549 (Fam)). In this case concerning a woman with learning disabilities, the court states that capacity requires an understanding of all the following:

■ The reason for contraception and what it does (which includes the likelihood of pregnancy if it is not in use during sexual intercourse).

■ The types of contraception available and how each is used.

■ The advantages and disadvantages of each type.

- The possible side effects of each and how they can be dealt with.

- How easily each type can be changed.

- The generally accepted effectiveness of each.

Excluded is any understanding of the consequences of the woman having a child. The judge in this case, Mr Justice Bodey, was clear on this point:

> *'I do not consider that questions need be asked as to the woman's understanding of what bringing up a child would be like in practice; nor any opinion attempted as to how she would be likely to get on; nor whether any child would be likely to be removed from her care.'*
> (A Local Authority v A [2010] EWHC 1549 (Fam))

Until the courts revisit the above guidance, this is the basis for the capacity assessment that needs to be undertaken before contraception can be provided on the basis of best interests. The responsibility for assessing the ability of a woman with learning disabilities to decide about contraception sits with the potential prescriber – most commonly a doctor. Indeed, Mr Justice Bodey suggested that the assessment should be common practice in GP surgeries and family planning clinics.

Women with learning disabilities are at risk of a poor decision-making process if they are assessed as either having or not having capacity to make decisions about their contraception. For example, a woman assessed as having capacity may be given a long-acting contraception without a reasonable understanding of the consequences or support to understand that she can change her mind about using contraception. Alternatively, a woman assessed as lacking capacity may have been denied her right to make her own decision, and any contraceptive used may not be in her best interests.

Contraception and best interests decision-making

In the case above, where the court ruled that it was not in the best interests of a woman with learning disabilities to be sterilised ([2013] EWHC 242 (COP)), it also ruled that it was not in her best interests to be prescribed contraception. She was found not to:

- have any period problems that contraception might help with

- be at risk of pregnancy, as she wasn't showing any interest in a sexual relationship and was supervised in the community.

The court ruled that there was no justification to subject her to the disadvantages and risks of any form of contraception. If contraception is argued to be in a woman's best interests in similar circumstances – 'just in case' a woman has sex with a man – it is strongly advised that the courts are asked to make a judgement. This would support the woman's rights by ensuring that those proposing (or providing) contraception are required to account for the possible divergence from case law.

Where a woman has been assessed as lacking capacity to decide about contraception, she may also lack capacity to consent to sex. Therefore, providing contraception in the best interests of a woman who may be having, or interested in having, sex, requires consideration as to whether the sex may be exploitative or abusive. It is recommended that the authority of the court is sought in such cases to, for example, ensure contraception is not being used as a convenient alternative to putting appropriate measures in place to protect a woman from sexual abuse.

As seen in the case where the court supported a vasectomy for a man with learning disabilities in his best interests, it is possible to lack capacity to make a decision about contraception while having capacity to consent to sex (NHS Trust v DE [2013] EWCH 2562).

If contraception is to be provided in a woman's best interests, principle 5 of the Mental Capacity Act (2005) requires a consideration of which method may be least restrictive. Sam Rowlands has been an expert witness to the Court of Protection addressing this specific issue in the case of [2013] EWHC 242 (COP). This case also helpfully considered the relative restrictiveness of different forms of contraception when addressing the requirement of principle 5 of the Mental Capacity Act (2005) to have regard to what may be least restrictive. Rowlands provided information regarding the effectiveness and restrictiveness of different options. He presented this analysis in an article which specifically addressed contraception decision-making for people with learning disabilities (Rowlands, 2011). His updated tables are reproduced here with permission (Table 3.1 & 3.2).

Table 3.1: Contraceptive methods in order of increasing effectiveness

Method	% of women experiencing an unintended pregnancy within the first year of use with typical use of the method
Condom	18
Pill/patch/ring	9
Injection	6
Copper intrauterine device (IUD)	0.8
Female sterilisation	0.5
Intrauterine system (IUS)	0.2
Implant	0.05

The shaded area indicates methods that have failure rates of less than 1%.

Reproduced with kind permission from Rowlands S (2011) Learning disability and contraceptive decision making. *Journal of Family Planning & Reproductive Health Care* **37** 173-78. Adapted from Trussell J (2011) Contraceptive failure in the United States. *Contraception* **83** 397-404.

Table 3.2: Methods of contraception in order of increasing restrictiveness of a person's rights and freedom of action

	Discontinuation possible by client	Potential hormonal side effects	Effect on menstruation	Duration of action	Formal procedure necessary for initiation	Risks of procedure	Further procedures needed for continuation
Condom	Yes	No	None	Transient	No	N/A	N/A
Combined hormonal (pill/patch)	Yes	Yes	Improved	Transient	No	N/A	N/A
Progestogen-only pill	Yes	Yes	Variable	Transient	No	N/A	N/A
Injection	Yes	Yes	Usually abolished	13 weeks*	Minor	Almost nil	As for initiation
Implant	Not normally	Yes	Often induces unscheduled bleeding	3 years	Yes**	Minor	Yes**
IUS	Not normally	Occasional – mild and only initially	Mirena usually abolishes it; Jaydess suppresses bleeding less	3-5 years	Yes**	Minor	Yes**
IUD	Not normally	No	May worsen	10 years	Yes**	Minor	Yes**
Sterilisation	No	No	None	Permanent	Yes**	Major (in comparison to reversible methods)	No

*Plus potential delay in return of fertility of up to one year.

**In all but mild cases of learning disability this will almost certainly necessitate general anaesthesia.

N/A = not applicable.

Reproduced with kind permission from Rowlands S (2011) Learning disability and contraceptive decision making. *Journal of Family Planning & Reproductive Health Care* **37** 173-78.

Recommended good practice: decisions on contraception and sterilisation for women with learning disabilities

- It should be clear whether the decision about contraception is made by the woman herself, or by the doctor in the woman's best interests.

- Where there are doubts about a woman's capacity to make a decision about contraception or sterilisation, the Court of Protection should be involved. This is particularly important if the treatment is to be provided for a woman who expresses a wish to have children.

- A decision regarding non-therapeutic sterilisation (i.e. where one goal is to prevent pregnancy rather than just addressing difficulties associated with menstruation) in a woman's best interests must be referred to the Court of Protection.

- Any use of contraception to avoid pregnancy in a woman's best interests should be referred to the Court of Protection.

- Where there are doubts about the therapeutic benefits (e.g. relieving difficulties associated with periods) of contraception or sterilisation proposed in a woman's best interests, the Court of Protection should be involved.

- Be alert to the risk of contraception hiding potential sexual abuse.

Case example: Seema

Seema is a 25-year-old woman with learning disabilities who lives with her mother. She has been involved in a woman's group run at the local college. The facilitator of the group is running a session on different kinds of contraception. During this session Seema realises that the implant she has in her upper arm is a contraceptive. The facilitator explores this with Seema. She says she was told by her mother, who took her to the doctor, that it was to 'stop her bleeding'. Because Seema said it was 'changed' recently, the facilitator understands that Seema has been using this contraceptive for several years (an implant can last for three years). Seema becomes increasingly upset with this realisation. She says she wants to have a baby and has a long-term boyfriend she wants to marry.

Has the Mental Capacity Act (2005) been followed in relation to the implant?

The clinicians who prescribed and inserted the implant should follow the Mental Capacity Act (2005). The decision to use contraception should be Seema's, unless she has been found to lack capacity to make this decision. If this is the case, a best interests decision needs to be made.

There are serious concerns here to suggest that the Mental Capacity Act (2005) has not been adhered to, regardless of Seema's capacity to make the decision. It seems unlikely that the clinicians assessed her as having capacity to consent to the contraception. She suggests she did not know what it was for, and if she had, she may not have consented to it, as she says she wants a baby.

For a best interests decision to be made, Seema needs to have been found to lack capacity to consent to contraception. The case discussed above sets out what the assessment should cover (A Local Authority v A [2010] EWHC 1549 (Fam)). Potentially, if given all possible support to make her own decision (as is required under principle 2 of the Act) Seema could make this choice herself, and so a best interests decision should not have been made.

If Seema is assessed as not having capacity to make the decision, her views should still be considered. As such, Seema, her mother and the doctor would potentially have conflicting ideas about what is in her best interests. This would be the kind of dispute that should be referred to the Court of Protection, which would then make a decision on her capacity and/or in her best interests.

There may also be an issue in the use of an implant in her best interest as there are less restrictive options for contraception available (referring to Sam Rowlands' table on p.56).

How should the concerns about the law not being followed be addressed?

The facilitator could explore with Seema what she would like to happen. Seema may, for example, come to understand the possible reasons why she was given contraception and accept its use – not wanting to upset her mother by disagreeing with her. Alternatively, she could be clear that she wants support to have the implant removed. Potentially, the facilitator will not be able to have further discussions with Seema, or sufficient discussions to be able to take a view on her capacity to make the relevant decisions. This could be because, for example, the session is about to end and/or it is difficult to arrange one-to-one time together.

A recommended option is to raise a safeguarding alert due to the possibility of Seema being unlawfully prescribed a medication which could have serious physical and emotional consequences. It may also have breached her right to family life under the European Convention on Human Rights.

If the use of contraception is ongoing and against Seema's wishes, her capacity to make a decision about the contraception or whether this is in her best interests should be tested in the Court of Protection. This application could be made by Seema, the facilitator or an advocate. However, the message from the Court of Protection (see LB Hillingdon v Steven Neary [2011] FWHC 1377, discussed above) is that the local authority should itself make an application to the Court of Protection – potentially as part of the safeguarding process. There is a similar expectation on the clinicians prescribing or administering the contraception to seek the authority of the Court of Protection.

Other options exist, including reporting the professionals involved to their regulatory bodies for not following the law, or helping Seema to access legal support to sue the same individuals. These may sound excessive, but what could be happening in this case is that Seema is being unlawfully denied her right to have children. This would be a form of eugenics made possible by modern contraceptive methods.

Decisions where a woman with learning disabilities is pregnant

Where a woman with learning disabilities is pregnant, decisions may arise in relation to two key areas:

- Abortion.
- Method of birth.

There no special rules set out in the Mental Capacity Act (2005) regarding these decisions. There are, however, strong arguments for seeing both as 'serious medical treatments' that require the safeguard of independent mental capacity advocates if a best interests decision is being made and there are no family members or friends who can adequately represent the woman.

In a small number of cases, the courts have been asked to make judgements in these two areas.

Termination

Abortion is a criminal offence unless certain criteria are met. These are set out in Section 1 of the Abortion Act (1967) (covering England, Wales and Scotland), as follows:

Medical termination of pregnancy:
1. Subject to the provisions of this section, a person shall not be guilty of an offence under the law relating to abortion when a pregnancy is terminated by a registered medical practitioner if two registered medical practitioners are of the opinion, formed in good faith –

   a. that the pregnancy has not exceeded its twenty-fourth week and that the continuance of the pregnancy would involve risk, greater than if the pregnancy were terminated, of injury to the physical or mental health of the pregnant woman or any existing children of her family; or

b. that the termination is necessary to prevent grave permanent injury to the physical or mental health of the pregnant woman; or

c. that the continuance of the pregnancy would involve risk to the life of the pregnant woman, greater than if the pregnancy were terminated; or

d. that there is a substantial risk that if the child were born it would suffer from such physical or mental abnormalities as to be seriously handicapped.

The Court of Protection has been asked to rule on individual women's capacity to consent to having an abortion. In one case, a woman with bipolar disorder was seeking an abortion prior to 24 weeks ([2013] EWCOP 1417). The medical staff had assessed her as lacking capacity to decide about this, so were petitioning the court to make a best interests decision. The judge ruled against the medical opinion and found her to have capacity to make her own decision. He noted the woman having consistently wanted an abortion. While some of her reasons for doing so were potentially associated with paranoid thoughts towards her husband and mother, she also provided rational reasons for wanting an abortion. This included her concerns about her ability to bring up a child.

A woman with learning disabilities reported to be in the 'bottom 1% of the population' intellectually was similarly found to have capacity to make a decision about her pregnancy ([2013] EWHC 50 (COP)). Her choice was to continue the pregnancy. Mr Justice Hedley cautioned against mixing the capacity assessment for a decision about continuing a pregnancy with the mother's ability to bring up a child. This reflects the judgements discussed above for assessing capacity to make decisions about having sex (D Borough Council v AB [2011] EWHC 101 (COP)) or using contraception (A Local Authority v A [2010] EWHC 1549 (Fam)).

Mr Justice Hedley in this case also recommended professionals to follow the guidance provided in a pre- Mental Capacity Act (2005) case ([2003] EWHC 2793 (Fam)) regarding when questions about potential terminations should be brought to the Court of Protection. This guidance stated that the Courts should be involved in any of the following circumstances:

i. Where there is a dispute as to capacity, or where there is a realistic prospect that the patient will regain capacity, following a response to treatment, within the period of her pregnancy or shortly thereafter;

ii. Where there is a lack of unanimity amongst the medical professionals as to the best interests of the patient;

iii. Where the procedures under Section 1 of the Abortion Act 1967 have not been followed (i.e., where two medical practitioners have not provided a certificate);

iv.   Where the patient, members of her immediate family, or the foetus' father have opposed, or expressed views inconsistent with, a termination of the pregnancy; or

v.   Where there are other exceptional circumstances (including where the termination may be the patient's last chance to bear a child).

(Mr Justice Coleridge, [2003] EWHC 2793 (Fam))

Method of birth

The courts have been called to make best interests decisions under the Mental Capacity Act (2005) as to how a pregnant woman should give birth. In all of the following cases the court ruled that the woman lacked capacity to make a decision about how to give birth, and it was in her best interests to have a caesarean section:

■   Re AA [2012] EWHC 4378 (COP): a woman with mental health needs pregnant with her third child. The previous two were born by caesarean section and were in care.

■   [2014] EWHC 132 (Fam): a woman with mental health needs pregnant with her first child.

■   [2014] EWCOP 11: a woman with autism and learning disabilities pregnant with her sixth child. The previous five had been taken into care.

■   [2014] EWCOP 30: a woman with mental health needs who thought those treating her were intending to harm her unborn child.

■   [2016] EWCOP 51: a woman with autism and learning disabilities thought to have undergone genital mutilation as child. She was reported to believe babies 'popped out'.

One of these cases ([2014] EWCOP 11) provides guidance on what the pregnant mother needs to understand in order to have capacity to decide on the method of birth. In this case the judge ruled that in order to have capacity to decide on the mode and timing of birth, the mother would need to understand the following:

i.   Ante-natal care and monitoring, including blood tests to check for anaemia and diabetes; urine tests to check for infections; the benefits of discussion with health services about delivery options;

ii.   Ante-natal monitoring of the foetus; the value of an ultra-sound imaging;

iii.   Mode of delivery of the baby, including vaginal delivery, and caesarean section;

iv.   Natural and/or induced labour;

v.   Anaesthesia and pain relief;

vi. The place of delivery – eg. at home or in a hospital – and the risks and benefits of each option;

vii. The risk of complications, arising from conditions relevant to the mother or the baby;

viii. Post-natal care of mother and baby.

(Mr Justice Cobb, [2014] EWCOP 11)

It is significant that none of the women were found to have capacity to make the decision regarding the method of birth in any of the cases listed above. This does raise the question of whether the courts are setting an overly demanding capacity assessment in this area.

When making a best interests decision about the method of birth, the law requires a singular focus on the interests of the woman and not the unborn child. The interests of the unborn child are only relevant in as much as these may impact on the woman, for example, how she would respond if the child died during labour.

When the court has found a caesarean to be in a woman's best interests, it can give the hospital the authority to restrain the woman to the extent of depriving her of her liberty (see, for example, [2016] EWCOP 51). This is to allow for the recommended monitoring, treatment and post-delivery care related to birth by caesarean section.

The courts have been very critical of those seeking the courts to make decisions about a mother's capacity and her best interests regarding method of birth late in the pregnancy (see, for example, [2016] EWCOP 51). The annex to [2014] EWCOP 30 provides guidance for heath trusts on making applications to the Court of Protection if a pregnant woman lacks, or may lack, capacity to make decisions about her obstetric care. This is reproduced in the Appendix. For general information about the rights of pregnant women to make decisions about their bodies see www.birthrights.org.uk/library/factsheets/Consenting-to-Treatment.pdf

The interests of the child of a person with learning disabilities

The Mental Capacity Act (2005) does not apply to those under 16. The interests of children are set out in the Children's Act (1989). This includes the process required if a child is to be removed from parental care. Where parents lack capacity to decide to relinquish their parental responsibilities under Section 20, or there is doubt as to whether they are providing informed consent, legal authority is required. This process is not always followed. For example, a couple with learning disabilities were awarded compensation after their child was, at birth, removed from their care for a year without the local authority having instigated care proceedings ([2014] EWFC 38; see also [2013] 2 FLR 987). The Mental Capacity Act (2005) specifically prohibits the following decisions being made on behalf of a parent with learning disabilities:

- discharging parental responsibility for a child in matters not relating to the child's property

- consenting to a child being placed for adoption or the making of an adoption order.

Chapter 4: The Sexual Offences Act (2003)

The Sexual Offences Act (2003) defines sexual crimes against adults and children. This chapter only examines potential offences against adults with learning disabilities (aged 16+). The age at which individuals are legally able to consent to sex is 16 regardless of the genders of the people involved.

A sexual offence will be committed against an adult with learning disabilities if the specific requirements of one or more offences are met. These fall into four distinct areas:

1. Universal sexual offences, which may be committed against anyone.

2. Specific offences against people with a 'mental disorder' (which includes people with learning disabilities).

3. 'Abuse of trust' offences, which apply when someone over the age of 18 who is in a position of trust has sex with a person under the age of 18 (for example, a teacher having sex with a 17-year-old student).

4. Prohibited family relationships (for example, a father having sex with his 21-year-old daughter).

At times there will be a choice as to which offence or offences an individual is charged with or prosecuted for. For example, a male care worker who is alleged to have had sex with a 16-year-old woman with learning disabilities could potentially be prosecuted under any of the first three areas above. The decision is made by the Crown Prosecution Service and will depend on a number of factors. This includes the likelihood of conviction and the potential sentence for each. Potentially, a decision will be made to prosecute against an offence which may attract a shorter sentence, because it may be more difficult to secure a conviction against a more 'serious' offence.

The importance of this decision is illustrated in a case that predated the Sexual Offences Act (2003). David Jenkins, a care worker, was charged with rape for having had sex with a woman with severe learning disabilities who became pregnant. He acknowledged sexual intercourse after DNA testing. Judge Simon Coltart rejected expert evidence suggesting the woman lacked capacity to consent to sex and Mr Jenkins was found not guilty. Subsequently, an alternative prosecution under the then offence of 'sex with a defective', which carried a lower maximum sentence, was not allowed (Dyer, 2000).

Universal sexual offences

The first four offences of the Sexual Offences Act (2003) can be committed against anyone; this includes children and adults. Conviction for these offences requires evidence of the victim not consenting and the perpetrator not reasonably believing they had consent. They are:

- rape, which is defined by a man inserting his penis into the mouth, anus or vagina of another person (s1)

- assault by penetration, which involves a woman or man inserting a body part or object into the mouth, anus or vagina of another person (s2)

- sexual assault, which is any sexual touching (s3)

- causing a person to engage in sexual activity with another person (s4).

Consent is defined in Section 74. It states: 'a person consents if he agrees by choice and has the freedom and capacity to make that choice. This is broken into two stages by the prosecution:

1. Whether the person had the capacity to make a choice about taking part in the sexual activity at the time. For example, a person may lack capacity due to a lack of sexual knowledge associated with their learning disability or because of being intoxicated from using alcohol or drugs.

2. Whether the person was in a position to make a choice freely. This is unlikely to be the case where violence was used or threatened (Crown Prosecution Service, 2017).

If a person with learning disabilities is assessed as lacking capacity to consent to sex under the Mental Capacity Act (2005) (using Mr Justice Mostyn's guidance discussed in Chapter 2) it is very likely that a prosecution would be successful under these universal offences. There would however need to be evidence of the sexual activity taking place (for example, DNA).

If a person with learning disabilities is assessed as having capacity to consent to sex under the Mental Capacity Act (2005), the prosecution will need to focus on the individual's ability to have made a choice at the time with the individual concerned. It may also examine the perception the accused person had of their consent. Potentially, a prosecution may be more likely under the specific offences against people with a mental disorder, which are described below. For example, it may be easier to show that a man was aware that a woman had learning disabilities and because of this was not in a position to refuse the sexual contact (Section 30), than it is to prove her inability to consent to the sexual contact which took place (Section 1).

Offences against people with a 'mental disorder'

The Sexual Offences Act (2003) includes specific sexual crimes against people with 'mental disorder' (Sections 30-44) to address additional vulnerabilities to sexual abuse. 'Mental disorder' is defined under Section 1 of the Mental Health Act (1983) as 'mental illness, arrested or incomplete development of mind, psychopathic disorder and any other disorder or disability of mind'. The definition includes people with learning disabilities. In 2016 there were 285 police-recorded sexual offences against people with mental disorder (Office for National Statistics, 2017).

This set of offences is grouped into three areas, outlined here.

Offences against persons with a mental disorder impeding choice

- Sexual activity with a person with a mental disorder impeding choice (s30).

- Causing or inciting a person, with a mental disorder impeding choice, to engage in sexual activity (s31).

- Engaging in sexual activity in the presence of a person with a mental disorder impeding choice (s32).

- Causing a person, with a mental disorder impeding choice, to watch a sexual act (s33).

For a conviction under these specific sections, the prosecution needs to show that the potential perpetrator 'knows or could reasonably be expected to know that [the person] has a mental disorder and that because of it or for a reason related to it [they are] likely to be unable to refuse'.

The person is unable to refuse if:

- they lack sufficient understanding of the nature, or reasonably foreseeable consequences of the sexual activity, or for any other reason, or

- they are unable to communicate their choice. (Section 30(2))

- The specific test for these sections of being 'unable to refuse' is different to the assessment of capacity to consent to sex under the general sexual offences above.

R. v C [2009] UKHL 42

This case has looked in detail at the meaning of being 'unable to refuse' because of, or for a reason related to, a mental disorder. It involved a man having sex with a woman with mental health needs. Initially, the man was charged with rape, but the charge was changed to a Section 30 offence: 'sexual activity with a person with a mental disorder impeding choice'. The High Court ultimately ruled that the woman was 'unable to refuse' the sexual contact because of her irrational fear of what might happen if she did. They found that for this reason she was 'unable to communicate' her choice.

The decision to prosecute under Section 30 could have been made because of a greater confidence in being able to prove an *inability to refuse* rather than a *lack of consent*. Also significant is the judges' guidance under Section 30 of consent being person- and situation-specific. That is, a person could consent to a sexual act with one person but not to the same sexual act with another. Thus, someone who is assessed as having capacity to consent to sex under the Mental Capacity Act (2005) could be found unable to refuse sex with a specific individual.

Inducements threats and deception

Sections 34-37 set out offences when a person with mental disorder is involved in sexual activity because of inducements, threats or a deception. This includes the perpetrator:

- having sex with the person (s34)
- causing them to have sex with someone else (s35)
- having sex in their presence (s36)
- making them view pornography or other sexual activity (s37).

Prosecution for each of these offences requires evidence of:

- the sexual activity taking place
- the potential perpetrator knowing, or it being reasonable to expect them to know, that the person had a mental disorder
- the person's agreement being obtained by an inducement offered or given, a threat made or a deception practised.

Potential offences under these sections include:

- a woman with learning disabilities having sex with a man who promises to marry her when he has no intention of doing so
- a man with learning disabilities having sex for a cigarette
- a woman with learning disabilities having sex with a man because he threatens to stop visiting.

Convictions under Sections 34–37 are extremely rare. For example, the figures for 2011 show no prosecutions for these, compared to the 22 convictions for the Section 30–33 offences *against persons with a mental disorder impeding choice* (Sentencing Council, 2012). It is unclear why this is the case. Potentially, crimes that could be prosecuted under these sections have been prosecuted under other offences. For example, in R v C [2009] UKHL 42, discussed above, the judgement suggested that a prosecution under Section 34 may have been easier than the conviction that was ultimately achieved under Section 30.

Another possible explanation is a poor awareness of Sections 34–37 among social care workers and the criminal justice system. Very often women with learning disabilities have sex with men without learning disabilities because of unfounded beliefs about where the relationship will lead. Where there is little doubt about the woman's consent (under general sexual offences or Section 30), prosecution under Section 34 could be considered as an option, for example, if the man suggests they will get married, go away on holiday together or have children, when the evidence does not support these being realistic expectations.

The maximum penalties for the offences in Sections 30–36 range between 10 years and life when penetration is involved.

Sexual abuse involving care workers

The remaining specific sexual offences against people with a mental disorder focus on abuse by care workers (Sections 38–44). They cover care workers:

- having sex with a person with a mental disorder (s38)

- making a person with a mental disorder have sex with another person (s39)

- for their sexual gratification, having sex in the presence of a person with a mental disorder (s40)

- for their sexual gratification, making a person with a mental disorder watch sexual activity or look at pornography (s41).

In Section 42 care workers are defined to include:

- staff who work in care homes

- healthcare providers

- workers and volunteers who have regular contact with the person because of their mental disorder.

The last of these groups is very broad and could apply to:

- taxi drivers who regularly take a person with learning disabilities to a day centre

- decorators at a group home

- caretakers or kitchen staff at a college

- volunteers at a social club for people with learning disabilities.

Prosecution for these offences requires evidence of the care relationship and the sexual activity. The person with a mental disorder's consent or otherwise is irrelevant. Maximum sentences for the different care worker offences range between seven and 14 years.

Sections 43 and 44 exclude from prosecution care workers who are in a pre-existing relationship with people with a mental disorder. This can be because of marriage or civil partnership, or the sexual relationship existing immediately prior to the care worker taking their role. These exceptions may be important where people with learning disabilities have voluntary or paid roles meeting the definition of care worker under Section 42. This could be, for example, where a woman with learning disabilities joins the board of a social club for people with learning disabilities that her wife attends, or, similarly, where a man with learning disabilities in a supported employment scheme regularly does gardening at his girlfriend's group home.

The care workers' offences address the potential for those supporting people with learning disabilities to abuse the dependence many of their clients may have on them. In 2011 there were just eight convictions under these sections (Sentencing Council, 2012).

Abuse of trust offences

There are a number of sexual offences that concern adults (aged 18+) having sex with those under 18 for whom they are in a position of trust. These are particularly relevant where the young person is 16 or over and may argue that they have consented to the sexual relationship. Common prosecutions in this category involve teachers having sex with their students. The law is communicating that whatever the young person's views about the sexual relationship, an offence is committed because the adult has taken advantage of a position of power.

The offences cover the same areas as those involving care workers:

- having sex with a person under 18 (s16)

- making a person under 18 have sex with another person (s17)

- for their sexual gratification, having sex in the presence of a person under 18 (s18)

- for their sexual gratification, making a person under 18 watch sexual activity or look at pornography (s19).

The occupations where the abuse of trust offences apply are set out in Section 21. They include education and training staff, workers in residential services, and health professionals. This list is not as comprehensive as the roles covered by the definition for care workers working with people with a mental disorder. For example, a taxi driver to a special school could not be prosecuted under the abuse of trust offences but could be under the abuse by care workers offences.

For abuse of trust offences, the prosecution must show that the adult did not have reasonable grounds to believe the young person was 18 or over.

The maximum penalty for abuse of trust offences is five years imprisonment. This is shorter than the maximums for all the offences involving people with a mental disorder, as well as those for the universal offences of rape and sexual assault. Consequently, it is unlikely that an adult in a position of trust who has sex with a person with learning disabilities (between the ages of 16 and 18) would be prosecuted under these specific offences.

Sex with adult relatives

Prior to the Sexual Offences Act (2003) there were restrictions on sex between genetically related women and men. These were the incest offences set out in the Sexual Offences Act (1956). One aim of these offences was to address the substantially increased risk of genetic disorders in children from parents who are closely biologically related.

The current Sexual Offences Act (2003) extended the range of prohibited family relationships in two significant ways: first, to include aunts, uncles, nieces and nephews; second, by including same-sex as well as opposite-sex relationships. Under Sections 64 and 65 it is illegal for someone to have sex involving penetration with an adult (aged 18+) who is their:

- parent
- grandparent
- child
- grandchild
- sister or brother
- aunt or uncle
- niece or nephew.

Penetration includes the insertion of a penis, body part or any other object into the anus, vagina or mouth. The maximum penalty for these offences is two years in jail. It is possible for both relatives to be prosecuted.

Including same-sex relatives means the current incest laws are not just about trying to avoid children being born to close relatives. It suggests a moral distaste for sex between relatives even if both are adults and fully consenting.

Cousins are not excluded from having sexual relationships. This is particularly relevant to services for people with learning disabilities, which may be seeing a significant number of children with learning disabilities born to cousins. For example, one study in Bradford found high rates of genetic disorders in children associated with cousin marriages within the Pakistani community (Sheridan *et al*, 2013).

Case example: potential offences

Concern has been expressed regarding the sexual behaviour of Peter, a 26-year-old man with severe learning disabilities. While he can understand some spoken language, he uses very few words and generally uses gestures and pointing to communicate his needs and wishes.

Individual work is set up for him. During one session he responds to images of sexual activity by miming being anally penetrated and names a male staff member from his residential service as the one doing it to him. After the session, it is learnt that this male staff member sometimes takes the man out alone when he is not working and buys him gifts.

At this stage, there is only an allegation. If the staff member has had sex with Peter, which sexual offences may have been committed?

Section 1: Rape

It will need to be shown that Peter did not consent. Either he did not agree by choice or he lacked the freedom and capacity to make that choice (Section 74).

Section 30: Sexual activity with a person with a mental disorder impeding choice

Because of the staff member's work at the residential service, it could be straightforward to show that he 'knows or could reasonably be expected to know' that Peter 'has a mental disorder and that because of it or for a reason related to it he is likely to be unable to refuse'. It would then need to be shown that Peter was unable to refuse because he lacked 'sufficient understanding of the nature, or reasonably foreseeable consequences of the sexual activity, or for any other reason', or he was 'unable to communicate his choice'.

Section 34: Inducement, threat or deception to procure sexual activity with a person with a mental disorder

It would be difficult for the staff member to suggest that it was not reasonable for him to know Peter had a mental disorder because of his work at the residential service. Taking Peter out and buying him gifts could count as an inducement, but it may need to be shown that this influenced Peter's reasons for having sex.

Section 38: Care worker having sex with a person with a mental disorder

Potentially, this would be the least challenging prosecution to secure, as the staff member is a care worker.

Evidence of sexual activity

Common to all the offences above is the need to provide convincing evidence of the staff member having sex with Peter in addition to what Peter communicated in the session. This could be:

- physical evidence of Peter recently having had anal sex
- DNA evidence that indicates sexual activity between the staff member and Peter, for example, the staff member's semen found in Peter's anus or on his clothes
- photographic evidence of sexual activity – if, for example, the staff member filmed the abuse or there is CCTV footage showing him taking Peter to a secluded place
- witnesses raising concerns about the relationship between the staff member and Peter.

The decision of whether Peter should have a forensic examination needs to be made under the Mental Capacity Act (2005) (see below).

Collecting forensic evidence

Where there are concerns that a sexual offence may have been committed involving a person with learning disabilities, there may be a need to collect forensic evidence. This may include:

- physical examination of the person, including their genitals
- pregnancy testing
- testing for sexually transmitted diseases
- taking swabs, internally and externally, which may reveal the potential perpetrator's DNA

■ examining clothing, bedding and other items for evidence of sexual activity, including DNA.

Even when conducted sensitively, forensic examinations can be traumatising. Whether or not to have a forensic examination should be the person's decision. Where the person lacks capacity to make this decision, a best interests decision needs to be made under the Mental Capacity Act (2005).

The timing of forensic examinations and for collecting other physical evidence is critical. Table 4.1 sets out timescales recommended by the Faculty of Forensic and Legal Medicine (2017).

Table 4.1: Recommended maximum sample collection times after an alleged incident

Area	Maximum time after incident
Fingernails	2 days unless unwashed then up to 7 days
Mouth (for semen from oral sex)	2 days
Hands and other areas of skin	2 days unless unwashed then up to 7 days
Vagina	7 days
Anus	3 days

Online sexual abuse and 'sexting'

Increasingly, people with learning disabilities may be involved in online/mobile phone sexual abuse. This may involve:

■ being encouraged to take explicit photos or videos of themselves

■ sending sexually explicit pictures of themselves to other people

■ receiving sexually explicit images

■ accessing illegal images, including child pornography

■ being groomed online for sexual abuse.

As with other sexual offences, people with learning disabilities could be either the victim or perpetrator of the related offences. The Sexual Offences Act (2003) covers some of these areas. This includes:

■ the offences against people with a mental disorder, detailed above, regarding being exposed to sexually explicit materials (sections 33, 37 and 41)

- Section 47, which makes it an offence to take, hold or distribute indecent images of children and young people up to the age of 18 – extending the Protection of Children Act (1978).

The grooming offences in the Sexual Offences Act (2003) only apply to grooming children under the age of 16 (sections 14 and 15).

Other relevant legislation

The Communications Act (2003) covers the whole of the UK. Section 127 makes it an offence to send electronic material which is 'grossly offensive or of an indecent, obscene or menacing character'.

The Malicious Communications Act (1988), (England and Wales) makes it an offence to send, electronically or by other means, materials which are indecent, offensive or threatening.

The Criminal Justice and Courts Act (2015) applies across the UK. It includes the offence of sharing sexual images of a person without their consent. It needs to be shown that the intention was to cause them distress (section 33).

A number of resources have been developed to support people with learning disabilities to understand the risks associated with sending and receiving explicit images and cyberbullying. These include:

- *Staying Safe on Social Media and Online*, produced by the Foundation for People with Learning Disabilities (2014): www.mentalhealth.org.uk/learning-disabilties/publications/staying-safe-social-media-and-online

- *Learning Disabilities, Autism and Internet Safety*: A Parent's Guide, produced by Cerebra (2015): http://w3.cerebra.org.uk/help-and-information/guides-for-parents/learning-disabilities-autism-and-internet-safety-a-parents-guide

Chapter 5: Marriage, civil partnership and forced marriages

A positive development in the lives of some people with learning disabilities has been the opportunity to get married or enter into a civil partnership. The minimum age for both is 16. The consent of a parent or guardian is required up to the age of 18 in England, Wales and Northern Ireland. This is not needed in Scotland.

Civil partnerships were introduced across the UK under the Civil Partnership Act (2004).They offered same-sex couples very similar rights and responsibilities as those gained through marriage. Since 2014 same-sex couples have also had the option to get married in the UK, apart from in Northern Ireland, under the Marriage (Same Sex Couples) Act (2013) and the Marriage and Civil Partnership (Scotland) Act (2014). The law does not allow opposite-sex couples to enter into a civil partnership, though this alternative to marriage is open to all in some other countries (for example, the Netherlands).

This chapter looks at the legal requirements for consent to marriage or civil partnership. There has been a growing recognition of people with learning disabilities being forced to marry, and so the legislation in this area is also included.

Marriage

Marriage, a ritual dating back over hundreds of years, is essentially an agreement between two people. The person conducting the ceremony must be authorised to do so, and there must be two other witnesses. There are also rules relating to when and where marriages can take place, as outlined in the Marriage Act (1994).

At times, the courts have been asked to rule on whether an individual was able to make this agreement. They continue to refer to cases from very different times – for example, a judgement in 1854 which found that individuals are married 'if they understand that by that act they have agreed to cohabit together and with no other person' (Harrod v Harrod (1854)).

The Mental Capacity Act (2005) explicitly excludes the possibility of making a best interests decision for someone to get married if they are unable to make this decision themselves (Section 27). Similarly, a best interests decision cannot be made for someone to enter into a civil partnership, or to agree to end a marriage or civil partnership after a two-year separation (Section 27).

Essentially, it is the responsibility of the person conducting the ceremony to be assured that both individuals are capable of understanding the contract they are entering into. The authorised person should not proceed with a marriage if they have doubts about the consent of either individual (General Register Office, 2015).

The courts carefully considered the issue of consent to marriage in the case of Sheffield City Council v E [2004] EWHC 2808 (Fam). The question was whether a 21-year-old woman with learning disabilities had the capacity to agree to marry a man who had a history of sexual and violent offences. Justice Munby made the following general points about the test of capacity to enter into a marriage:

- It is not about understanding the implications of marriage with a particular individual.

- It should not be a judgement on the wisdom of the decision.

- It does not require a person to be able to look after their own property and affairs.

- The bar should not be set too high and so deny many people with learning disabilities the potential pleasures of marriage.

He went on to provide the legal capacity test for marriage (see box below).

Capacity to marry

It is not enough that someone appreciates that he or she is taking part in a marriage ceremony or understand its words.

He or she must understand the nature of the marriage contract.

This means that he or she must be mentally capable of understanding the duties and responsibilities that normally attach to marriage.

That said, the contract of marriage is in essence a simple one, which does not require a high degree of intelligence to comprehend. The contract of marriage can readily be understood by anyone of normal intelligence.

There are thus, in essence, two aspects to the inquiry whether someone has capacity to marry:

1. Does he or she understand the nature of the marriage contract?

2. Does he or she understand the duties and responsibilities that normally attach to marriage?

The duties and responsibilities that normally attach to marriage can be summarised as follows:

a. Marriage, whether civil or religious, is a contract, formally entered into.

b. It confers on the parties the status of husband and wife, the essence of the contract being an agreement between a man and a woman to live together, and to love one another as husband and wife, to the exclusion of all others.

c. It creates a relationship of mutual and reciprocal obligations, typically involving the sharing of a common home and a common domestic life and the right to enjoy each other's society, comfort and assistance.

Source: Mr Justice Munby, Sheffield City Council v E [2004] EWHC 2808 (Fam)

The outcome of this important case was that the woman was found to have capacity to consent to marriage. In advance of the hearing, Sheffield City Council used the *inherent jurisdiction* of the courts to prevent the marriage taking place prior to a decision on her capacity. The forced marriage legislation set out overleaf provides alternative ways of preventing a marriage taking place where there are concerns about the ability of one of the parties to consent. This section also shows how marriages can be found invalid after the event.

Mr Justice Munby's capacity assessment could be used as a guide to support people with learning disabilities' understanding of marriage and help prepare those individuals planning to get married. It was produced before same-sex marriage became legal, so the duties and responsibilities would need to similarly apply for two wives or two husbands. The expectation to love one another 'to the exclusion of others' may be interpreted differently by different people. Often married people have sex with other people either with or without their spouse's consent.

Civil partnership

As for marriage, the law also sets out who is authorised to conduct civil partnership ceremonies and the need for two witnesses (Civil Partnership Act (2004)). There are also restrictions on where they can take place. This includes some prohibition of civil partnerships taking place within religious premises – restrictions that similarly apply to same-sex marriages.

The person who is authorised to register civil partnerships should not proceed with the registration if they have concerns about the consent of those involved. As for marriage, a civil partnership may be declared void or voidable under a nullity order made by a court. If it is declared void it is treated as if it never existed. Where it is declared voidable the civil partnership existed until the date on which the order is made final. The Civil Partnership Act (2014) states that a civil partnership between two women or two men may be voidable if:

- *'either of them did not validly consent to its formation (whether as a result of duress, mistake, unsoundness of mind or otherwise)*

- *at the time of its formation either of them, though capable of giving a valid consent, was suffering (whether continuously or intermittently) from mental disorder of such a kind or to such an extent as to be unfitted for civil partnership'.* (Section 50)

While the first of these conditions is understandable, the second is very controversial. It is difficult to understand how someone able to give valid consent can at the same time be 'unfitted for civil partnership'. At the time of writing no case law could be identified regarding voiding a civil partnership for these reasons.

Forced marriages

The UK government defines forced marriage as:

> *'A marriage in which one or both spouses do not consent to the marriage but are coerced into it. Duress can include physical, psychological, financial, sexual and emotional pressure. In the cases of some vulnerable adults who lack the capacity to consent, coercion is not required for a marriage to be forced.'* (Cabinet Office, 2014, p5).

Forced marriages are often associated with other forms of abuse, including financial and sexual. For example, often a person who is forced to get married will be made to have sex that they do not consent to, or that they lack the capacity to consent to. Sexual offences legislation has moved on from suggesting that there can be no rape within marriage.

Forced marriages take place for a wide range of reasons including:

- to comply with agreements made by other family members, for example, promises for children to marry particular individuals when they get older

- to maintain the cultural or religious heritage of a family

- to access immigration rights

- to maintain or improve the financial position of a family or individual

- particularly when women are forced to marry, to gain a carer for their husband or other family member

- to address the 'shame' an individual has brought the family, for example, by having a relationship with someone outside of the family's community

- to control a family member who may be lesbian or gay.

Arranged marriages are very different to forced marriages. While family members may suggest the spouse, the consent of both is required in an arranged marriage.

The UK's Foreign and Commonwealth Office has a Forced Marriage Unit (see Resources). This provides support to people who may be at risk of entering or are in a forced marriage. This service is available 24 hours a day to address forced marriages that could take place in the UK or anywhere around the world where British residents are involved. Often Foreign Office staff overseas will be called to prevent marriages taking place or to assist the return of a UK resident facing a forced marriage.

The Forced Marriage Unit produces annual statistics. The figures for 2016 show that it was involved in 1,428 cases of possible forced marriage that year (Home Office, 2017). For each, just one potential 'victim' is identified, although it is possible for both partners to be forced to marry each other. The majority (80%) of the victims were women; 2% of victims were known to identify as lesbian, gay or transgender.

Where possible, a 'focus country' was identified in the 2016 figures. This is the country where a potential spouse was residing, or where the forced marriage was due to take place. Only 11% of cases were classed as 'domestic' – where both people were living in the UK and this was where the marriage was to take place. The most common focus countries were Pakistan (43%), Bangladesh (8%), India (6%), Somalia (3%) and Afghanistan (3%). Another 80 countries were associated with forced marriages in this research. In 9% of cases the focus country was unknown.

While forced marriage has been traditionally understood as happening between a woman and a man, the possibility exists for forced same-sex marriages or civil partnerships. There is no evidence of these in the 2016 statistics. This can be partly understood because same-sex marriage or civil partnerships do not exist in many of the focus countries. For example, in Pakistan, Bangladesh and India same-sex relationships continue to be illegal.

People with learning disabilities were involved in 140 (10%) of the cases in 2016, despite making up just 2% of the population (Foundation for People with Learning Disabilities, undated). The majority of victims with learning disabilities were men (61%). Indeed, 32% of all male victims have learning disabilities, compared to just 4% of all the women victims.

The author's experience of meeting several men with learning disabilities in forced marriages is that their wives were extremely vulnerable themselves. They had been married overseas and were living with the man and his family with little opportunity to make decisions, access money or learn English.

Table 5.1 gives the age profile of the victims with learning disabilities compared to the other victims. It shows that people with learning disabilities are generally older than other people who are forced to marry.

Table 5.1: Age of victims of forced marriage

Age of victim	People with learning disabilities, n = 140 (%)	Other victims, n = 1,288 (%)
Under 18	5 (4%)	366 (28%)
18–21	19 (14%)	271 (21%)
22–25	30 (21%)	177 (14%)
26–30	27 (19%)	110 (9%)
31–40	29 (20%)	62 (5%)
41+	12 (9%)	16 (1%)
Unknown	18 (13%)	286 (22%)

Table 5.2: Focus country of victims of forced marriage

Focus country	People with learning disabilities, n = 140 (%)	Other victims, n = 1,288 (%)
UK (domestic)	10 (7%)	147 (11%)
Pakistan	88 (63%)	524 (41%)
Bangladesh	13 (9%)	108 (8%)
India	11 (8%)	68 (5%)
Other	12 (9%)	315 (24%)
Unknown	6 (4%)	126 (10%)

Table 5.2 compares the focus countries of people with learning disabilities with other victims. It shows that Pakistan is the country most commonly associated with forced marriages for both those victims with learning disabilities and the other victims, making up 63% and 41% of cases respectively. The difference

between these two figures is statistically significant ($p < 0.01$). This means that there is a particular risk for people with learning disabilities in Pakistani communities being forced to marry.

Legal cases involving people with learning disabilities

Cases of potentially forced marriage involving people with learning disabilities have reached the courts. These give some insight into the context and ways in which people with learning disabilities may experience a forced marriage.

Re SA [2005] EWHC 2942 (Fam)

This case involved a young woman in the Pakistani community. She was profoundly deaf and communicated through British Sign Language – a language neither of her parents understood. An application was made to court because of concerns that she may be forced to marry a man chosen by her family in Pakistan. There were also concerns about the possibility of her not being able to return to the UK if, for example, her husband was denied a visa to travel to the UK. The woman was assessed as both having capacity and wanting to get married. However, she was found not to understand the residency issues of marrying a man in Pakistan, and the implications this could have for her.

The court used its inherent jurisdiction to make an order putting very strict conditions on the possibility of marrying in Pakistan. This included her having the opportunity to return to live in her home town within four months of the marriage whether or not her husband was granted immigration clearance.

KC v City of Westminster Social and Community Services Department [2008] EWCA Civ 198

A man with severe learning disabilities had been married over the phone to a woman in Bangladesh. He lacked capacity to consent to marriage. Although the marriage was recognised in Bangladesh, the courts ruled that it was not recognised in the UK.

XCC v AA & Others [2012] EWHC 2183 (COP)

The Court of Protection was asked to make a ruling about a woman with severe learning disabilities living in the UK. She had been married to a man in Bangladesh with the support of her family. In addition to being assessed as lacking capacity to consent to marriage, she was found to lack capacity to consent to sex or to make decisions about her care. There was also evidence of her husband physically assaulting her. The judge found the husband's motivations for marrying her were limited to gaining entry to the UK. The finding was that the marriage was not recognised in the UK.

The judge was very critical of a number of medical professionals who on three separate occasions took no action to protect the woman when they were asked by the woman's family members to give her a pregnancy test. The judge said the concerns about her capacity in regard to marriage and pregnancy would have been obvious. He went on to suggest that professionals have a duty to report suspected forced marriages.

Sandwell vs RG and Others [2013] EWHC 2373 (COP)

The Court of Protection was similarly asked to rule on a marriage involving a man with learning disabilities and challenging behaviour who lived in residential care. The man's father arranged the wedding to a woman with physical disabilities in India. She said she was initially shocked when she met him on the wedding day in 2009, but agreed to go through with the wedding. She moved to the UK the following year and regularly saw her husband as well as having a sexual relationship with him.

The court heard that the man lacked capacity to consent to marriage or to have a sexual relationship. Unlike in the case above, the judge decided it was not in the man's best interests to annul the marriage. However, his wife was instructed not to have sex with him, as this would be a sexual offence.

Legal strategies to prevent forced marriages

The UK government has introduced legislation to try to address the problem of forced marriages.

Forced marriage protection orders

The Forced Marriage (Civil Protection) Act (2007) covers England, Wales and Northern Ireland. It provides the courts with powers intended to protect a person facing a forced marriage or who has been forced into marriage. For example, the court could order:

- a relative to hand over the potential victim's passport to prevent travel overseas for a possible marriage ceremony

- the whereabouts of the potential victim to be disclosed

- no contact between a wife who has been forced to marry and her husband or other family members.

In the first quarter of 2017, 47 applications were made for Forced Marriage Protection Orders, resulting in 49 orders (Ministry of Justice, 2017). The majority of these (62%) were concerned with protecting children and young people under the age of 18. There are currently no published statistics identifying how many people with learning disabilities are covered by these orders.

Anyone, including staff working with people with learning disabilities, can make an application for a Forced Marriage Protection Order. HM Courts and Tribunal Service has produced a helpful guide on how to do this (HM Courts and Tribunal Service, undated).

The Anti-social Behaviour, Crime and Policing Act (2014)

Further measures to address forced marriages are contained in the Anti-social Behaviour, Crime and Policing Act (2014). The act made breaching a Forced Marriage Protection Order a criminal offence punishable by up to five years in prison (Section 120). In addition, it introduced new crimes covering England, Wales and Scotland (Sections 121 & 122). These are:

- using violence, threats or coercion to force a person to marry

- facilitating the marriage of a person unable to consent to marriage – there is no requirement to show coercion

- taking someone out of the UK with the intention of forcing them to marry – whether or not the marriage takes place.

Only one prosecution has been reported to date (BBC News, 2015). This did not involve a person with learning disabilities.

Guidance for professionals

The government has developed multi-agency statutory guidance for dealing with forced marriage (Cabinet Office, 2014a). This includes step-by-step guidance for professionals handling cases (Cabinet Office, 2014b). It identifies a range of potential indicators for forced marriage. For people with learning disabilities this could include:

- being withdrawn from school or a day centre without explanation

- making an unusual trip outside of the country, for example, if the person with learning disabilities has never previously been taken back to the country of their family's origin

- staff being asked to sign a passport or visa application

- the person talking about marriage, jewellery or wedding clothes

- medical staff being asked to investigate a person's fertility.

The guidance talks about the 'one chance rule': there may be just once chance to speak to a person, to prevent a forced marriage or even to save their life. It requires professionals to act on concerns using the resources available to them – including children's and adults' safeguarding processes and the law.

Case example: Ghazala

Gail teaches in a local school for people with learning disabilities. While shopping in town she sees Ghazala, whom she used to teach until she left school eight years ago. Ghazala is sat by herself in a large fast-food restaurant. Gail assumes she is waiting for someone, as she would be unlikely to be out on her own due to the level of her learning disability and her Pakistani family's expectations for young women. Gail has not seen Ghazala since she finished school and hasn't heard anything of her since then. One reason for this is that Ghazala did not go on to study at the local college like her classmates. She was aware her family were keen to support Ghazala themselves at home.

Ghazala also sees Gail and waves to her. Gail goes to say hello and Ghazala excitedly tells her she is going on holiday to get married. Gail is very surprised to hear this because her level of learning disability suggests that she would lack capacity to get married. Gail asks who she is getting married to, and Ghazala says she doesn't know. This all happens in less than a minute, before a man – who Gail assumes is a male relative – arrives and hurries Ghazala out of the restaurant. He makes it very clear that he does not want to talk to Gail.

Gail reflects on what has happened. Her memory of Ghazala makes her doubt she has made up the marriage plan. She also thinks the man who arrived might have heard Ghazala mention marriage.

How should Gail respond?

Gail may be tempted to disregard the situation. Possibly, she may justify this because she no longer works with Ghazala and is concerned about 'interfering' in a family from a different culture to her own. She may also be concerned that any action taken could make things more difficult for Ghazala. Potentially, it could cause a lot of stress for the family when there may not even be a marriage planned for Ghazala.

Alternatively, Gail could respond formally to what could be a forced marriage.

Ideally, Gail would raise an adult safeguarding alert with the local authority. She may also want to speak to the Forced Marriage Unit for advice. She can do this 24 hours a day by phone (020 7008 0151).

Gail should not try to contact the family directly, as this may put Ghazala at greater risk.

What action could be taken by the local authority or the Forced Marriage Unit

Following the 'one chance rule', the local authority may decide that Gail's report raises enough of a concern to immediately apply to the courts for a Forced Marriage Protection Order. In this case it would be appropriate for the order to require the family to hand over Ghazala's passport to prevent her being taken out of the country. This could prevent both a forced marriage and sexual abuse.

If Gail's concerns are validated, work should be done with Gail's family to help them understand the requirement for consent to marriage in the UK. This could include the potential consequences – under the Anti-social Behaviour, Crime and Policing Act (2014) – for any person who facilitates a forced marriage.

Ideally, work would also take place with Ghazala which could:

- help her to understand why the formal response took place
- assess her capacity to consent to marriage –the marriage could potentially go ahead if she has capacity, or can be supported to gain capacity, to get married
- provide support to help her deal with any retribution from her family that she may experience
- offer her safe accommodation away from her family.

References and resources

Abbott D & Howarth J (2005) *Secret Loves, Hidden Lives? Exploring Issues For People With Learning Difficulties Who Are Gay, Lesbian or Bisexual*. Bristol: Policy Press.

BBC News (2015) *Forced Marriage Jail First as Cardiff Man Sentenced* [online]. Available at: /www.bbc.com/news/uk-wales-33076323 (accessed 3/9/17).

Cabinet Office (2014a) *The Right to Choose: Multi-agency statutory guidance for dealing with forced marriage* [online]. Available at: https://www.gov.uk/government/uploads/system/uploads/attachment_data/file/322310/HMG_Statutory_Guidance_publication_180614_Final.pdf (accessed 3/9/17).

Cabinet Office (2014b) *Multi-agency Practice Guidelines: Handling cases of forced marriage* [online]. Available at: https://www.gov.uk/government/uploads/system/uploads/attachment_data/file/322307/HMG_MULTI_AGENCY_PRACTICE_GUIDELINES_v1_180614_FINAL.pdf (accessed 3/9/17).

Cerebra (2015) *Learning Disabilities, Autism and Internet Safety: A parent's guide* [online]. Available at: http://w3.cerebra.org.uk/help-and-information/guides-for-parents/learning-disabilities-autism-and-internet-safety-a-parents-guide (accessed 3/9/17).

Chapman R, Ledger S & Townson L, with Docherty D (2015) *Sexuality and Relationships in the Lives of People with Intellectual Disabilities: Standing in my shoes*. London: Jessica Kingsley Publishers.

Crown Prosecution Service (2017) *Sexual Offences: Fact Sheet* [online]. Available at: www.cps.gov.uk/news/fact_sheets/sexual_offences (accessed 3/9/17).

Department of Health (2010) *Briefing on Mental Capacity Act Deprivation of Liberty Safeguards: April 2010* (Gateway reference: 14353) [online]. https://www.yourcareyoursupportwiltshire.org.uk/media/15630/dep-of-liberty-safeguards.pdf (accessed 27/8/17).

Dyer C (2000) Care worker's release on rape charge prompts CPS to seek review of law. *The Guardian* 24 January.

Faculty of Forensic and Legal Medicine (2017) *Recommendations for the Collection of Forensic Specimens from Complainants and Suspects* [online]. Available at: https://www.fflm.ac.uk/wp-content/uploads/2017/01/Recommendations-for-the-collection-of-forensic-specimens-from-complainants-and-suspects-FSSC-Jan-2017.pdf (accessed 3/9/17).

Foundation for People with Learning Disabilities (2014) *Staying Safe on Social Media and Online* [online]. Available at: https://www.mentalhealth.org.uk/learning-disabilties/publications/staying-safe-social-media-and-online (accessed 3/9/17).

Foundation for People with Learning Disabilities (undated) *Learning Disability Statistics* [online]. Available at: https://www.mentalhealth.org.uk/learning-disabilities/help-information/learning-disability-statistics- (accessed 3/9/17).

General Register Office (2015) *A Guide for Authorised Persons* [online]. Available at: https://www.gov.uk/government/uploads/system/uploads/attachment_data/file/408482/APsGuideFebruary15final.pdf (accessed 3/9/17).

Home Office (2016) *Mandatory reporting of Female Genital Mutilation: Procedural information* [online]. Available at: https://www.gov.uk/government/uploads/system/uploads/attachment_data/file/573782/FGM_Mandatory_Reporting_-_procedural_information_nov16_FINAL.pdf (accessed 3/9/17).

HM Courts and Tribunal Service (undated) *Forced Marriage Protection Orders: How can they protect me?* [online]. Available at: http://formfinder.hmctsformfinder.justice.gov.uk/fl701-eng.pdf (accessed 3/9/17).

Home Office (2017) *Forced Marriage Unit Statistics 2016* [online]. Available at: https://www.gov.uk/government/uploads/system/uploads/attachment_data/file/597869/Forced_Marriage_Unit_statistics-_2016.pdf (accessed 3/9/17).

Law Commission (2017) *Mental Capacity and Deprivation of Liberty* [online]. Available at: www.lawcom.gov.uk/wp-content/uploads/2017/03/lc372_mental_capacity.pdf (accessed 13/11/17).

McCarthy M (1999) *Sexuality and Women with Learning Disabilities*. London: Jessica Kinsley Publishers.

McCarthy M (2010) Exercising choice and control – women with learning disabilities and contraception. *British Journal of Learning Disabilities* **38** 293–302.

McCarthy M & Thompson D (1996) Sexual abuse by design: An examination of the issues in learning disability services. *Disability and Society* **11** (2) 205–217.

McCarthy M & Thompson D (2016) *Sex and the 3 Rs: Rights, responsibilities and risks* (4th edition). Brighton: Pavilion Publishing.

Ministry of Justice (2017) *Family Court Statistics Quarterly, England and Wales, January to March 2017* [online]. https://www.gov.uk/government/uploads/system/uploads/attachment_data/file/638330/fcsq-jan-march_2017.pdf (accessed 3/9/17).

Office for National Statistics (2017) *Crime in England and Wales: Appendix tables* [online]. https://www.ons.gov.uk/peoplepopulationandcommunity/crimeandjustice/datasets/crimeinenglandandwalesappendixtables (accessed 3/917).

Rowlands S (2011) Learning disability and contraceptive decision-making. *Journal of Family Planning and Reproductive Health Care* **37** (3) 173–178.

Rowlands S & Sam JJ (2018) Sterilization of those with intellectual disability.: evolution from non-consensual interventions to strict safeguards. *Journal of Intellectual Disabilities*. DOI:10.1177/1744629517747162.

SCIE (2011) *Good Practice Guidance on Accessing the Court of Protection* [online]. Available at: www.scie.org.uk/publications/guides/guide42/ (accessed 27/8/17).

Sentencing Council (2012) S*exual Offences Analysis and Research Bulletin* [online]. www.sentencingcouncil.org.uk/publications/item/sexual-offences-analysis-and-research-bulletin (accessed 3/9/2017).

Sheridan E, Wright J, Small N, Corry P, Oddie S, Whibley C, Petherick E, Malik T, Pawson N, McKinney P & Parslow R (2013) Risk factors for congenital anomaly in a multiethnic birth cohort: An analysis of the Born in Bradford study. *The Lancet* **382** (9901) 1350–1359.

Thompson D (2001) Is sex a good thing for men with learning disabilities? *Tizard Learning Disability Review* **6** (2) 4–12.

Williams R (2010) Mate crime fears for people with learning disabilities. *The Guardian* **14** September.

Court judgements

39 Essex Chambers: www.39essex.com
39 Essex Chambers is a legal practice that publishes a monthly newsletter on cases in the Court of Protection. It also provides updates of the mental capacity legislation in Scotland.

BAILII (British and Irish Legal Information Institute): www.bailii.org
Judgements of court cases across the UK, including those referred to the Court of Protection, are published freely online by the British and Irish Legal Information Institute.

Resources and organisations

Richard's Story: www.scie.org.uk/lgbtqi/video-stories/learning-disabilities
A Social Care TV film about a gay man with learning disabilities.

Home Office Forced Marriage Unit: https://www.gov.uk/guidance/forced-marriage
The Forced Marriage Unit (FMU) works both inside the UK, where support is provided to any individual, and overseas, where consular assistance is provided to British nationals, including dual nationals. It has a 24-hour public helpline to provide advice and support to victims of forced marriage as well as to professionals dealing with cases.

FPA specialist sexual health services for people with learning disabilities: www.fpa.org.uk/what-we-do/specialist-sexual-health-services-people-learning-disabilities
FPA works directly with people with learning disabilities in schools and other settings. It also facilitates workshops for family carers, and training and consultancy for professionals and frontline staff. It has a range of resources to support people with learning disabilities.

Image in Action: www.imageinaction.org
Image in Action has been providing sex education to people with learning disabilities for over 27 years. It also provides resources and support for professionals and families.

Respond: www.respond.org.uk
Respond works with children and adults with learning disabilities who have experienced abuse or trauma, as well as those who have abused others, through psychotherapy, advocacy, campaigning and other support. Respond also aims to prevent abuse by providing training, consultancy and research.

Birthrights *Consenting to Treatment* factsheet: www.birthrights.org.uk/library/factsheet/consenting-to-Treatment.pdf
General information about the rights of pregnant women to make decisions about their bodies.

Appendix

Guidance for decision-making for a pregnant woman who may lack capacity to make decisions about her antenatal, perinatal and postnatal care

This guidance was provided in the Annex to NHS Trust and others v FG [2014] EWCOP 30

Guidance

Introduction

1. In this guidance the following terminology will be used:

    'P'
    the pregnant woman who lacks, or may lack, the capacity to take decisions in relation to her antenatal, perinatal and postnatal care as a result of an impairment of, or a disturbance in, the functioning of her mind or brain resulting from her psychiatric illness;

    'obstetric care'
    all care and treatment needs brought about by P's pregnancy including antenatal care, management of labour and delivery, and postnatal care;

    'Mental Health Trust'
    the NHS Trust responsible for P's psychiatric care, whether in the community or in a psychiatric hospital;

    'psychiatric hospital'
    any mental health unit at which P resides, whether detained pursuant to statutory powers or as a voluntary patient;

'acute hospital'
a hospital other than the psychiatric hospital at which it is intended that P will receive obstetric care and deliver her child;

'Acute Trust'
the NHS Trust responsible for the acute hospital;

'Court'
either the Court of Protection or the Family Division of the High Court.

2. This Guidance applies in cases where a pregnant woman who lacks, or may lack, the capacity to make decisions about her obstetric care (see paragraph 1 above) resulting from a diagnosed psychiatric illness, falls within one of the four categories of cases set out in paragraph 3 below.

3. An Acute Trust and/or Mental Health Trust should make an application to seek orders in relation to P's obstetric care to the Court of Protection or to the Family Division of the High Court if the case falls within any of the following four categories, namely where:

    Category 1 – the interventions proposed by the Trust(s) probably amount to serious medical treatment within the meaning of COP Practice Direction 9E, irrespective of whether it is contemplated that the obstetric treatment would otherwise be provided under the MCA or MHA; or

    Category 2 – there is a real risk that P will be subject to more than transient forcible restraint; or

    Category 3 – there is a serious dispute as to what obstetric care is in P's best interests whether as between the clinicians caring for P, or between the clinicians and P and/or those whose views must be taken into account under s.4(7) of the MCA; or

    Category 4 – there is a real risk that P will suffer a deprivation of her liberty which, absent a Court order which has the effect of authorising it, would otherwise be unlawful (i.e. not authorised under s4B of or Schedule A1 to the MCA).

4. In relation to category 1, it is recommended that the following categories of case should be the subject of an application to the court, namely:

    i.   delivery by caesarean section is proposed in circumstances where the merits of that proposal are finely balanced; or

     i.   delivery by caesarean section is proposed and is likely to involve more than transient forcible restraint of P.

5.   It may be appropriate to make an application to the court in cases which do not fall within the categories set out in paragraph 3 above; it will depend on the facts of the case. If an application is so made, the provisions of this Guidance should be followed.

Assessment

6.   The early identification of an individual in respect of whom an application might have to be made is essential. In the case where P is detained under the provisions of the Mental Health Act (1983), the lead professional is likely to be a treating psychiatrist at the hospital where P is detained. In the case where P is living in the community the lead professional is likely to be a member of P's midwifery team.

7.   Once P has been so identified, the Acute and Mental Health Trusts should liaise to assess P's capacity to make decisions in respect of her obstetric care and to plan how and when such care is to be delivered in her best interests.

8.   An assessment of P's capacity to litigate should be undertaken; this will usually be performed by P's treating psychiatrist.

9.   Capacity may, of course, fluctuate and it is extremely important to keep the issue of capacity under regular review.

10. Where there are concerns about P's ability to care for her unborn child the Acute and/or Mental Health Trusts should notify the relevant social services department of P's case if social workers are not already involved with her. The local authority should commence child protection procedures immediately upon receipt of a referral. Thereafter, there should be regular liaison and co-operation between the Acute Trust, the Mental Health Trust and the local authority.

11. The Acute and Mental Health Trusts, together with the relevant local authority, should hold regular planning and review meetings ('professionals meetings'). Those meetings should be minuted. Multi-agency co-operation is likely to be an essential feature of the planning process to achieve the best outcome for P and her unborn child.

12. An identified clinician from the Acute Trust or the Mental Health Trust should be appointed to chair the planning and review meetings.

13. Part of the planning process should involve identifying whether and, if so, when a decision by the Court will be required to authorise obstetric care or any deprivation of liberty to facilitate its provision.

14. The planning process should include consideration of an assessment of the risk of harm, if any, which P poses to herself, to her unborn child or to others. Where any professional considers such a risk exists that assessment must be recorded in writing and presented at the next professionals meeting.

15. If as a result of the risk assessment the local authority proposes to make an application under the inherent jurisdiction for permission to withhold the care plan for the unborn child from P, the application should be made, save in the case of a genuine emergency, no later than four weeks before the expected date of delivery. (The threshold for the granting of such an application is high and applications will not be granted routinely).

16. If an application is made by either the Trusts or by the local authority for permission not to notify P of the application(s) and it is thought appropriate to apply for a Reporting Restrictions Order, the applicant(s) must give full and proper notice to the print and broadcast media of the same.

17. A decision by one agency to withhold information from any other agency must be recorded identifying the cogent reasons for the decision. The agency, from whom information is to be withheld, must be notified of the same at the earliest opportunity.

Application

18. Where it is decided that P's case falls within one of the four categories set out in paragraph 3 above or it is otherwise decided to make an application, an application should be made to the court at the earliest opportunity.

19. Save in a case of genuine medical emergency, any application should be made no later than four weeks before the expected date of delivery. This time frame is required for the following reasons:

    i.   where P is assessed as lacking capacity to litigate, it will enable the Official Solicitor to undertake any necessary investigations;

    ii. to ensure the final hearing is listed and heard at least a few days before the proposed interventions; and

    iii. to enable a directions hearing to be held around two weeks before the final hearing. The court and the parties will then have the opportunity to ensure the court has all the relevant and necessary evidence at the final hearing.

20. In compliance with the timetable set out above, the Trusts should in a timely manner, take the following steps:

    i.   issue the application

    ii. notify the Official Solicitor of the application;

iii. disclose any evidence to the Official Solicitor which they consider appropriate;

iv. seek an urgent directions hearing, preferably around two weeks before the final hearing, at which disclosure and the scope of the evidence can be determined;

v. liaise with the Clerk of the Rules to list the substantive hearing at an early stage.

21. It is important that the Trusts should seek early advice and input from their legal advisers.

22. Late applications are to be avoided save in a case of genuine medical emergency. They have four very undesirable consequences:

i. the application is more likely to be dealt with by the out of hours judge and without a full hearing in public;

ii. the available written evidence is more likely to be incomplete and necessitate substantial oral evidence;

iii. it seriously undermines the role that the Official Solicitor can and should properly play in the proceedings; and

iv. it deprives the court of the opportunity to direct that further evidence, including independent expert evidence, if necessary, is obtained in relation to the issue of capacity or best interests.

This approach is dictated by P's Article 5, 6 and 8 rights and best interests.

23. The following evidence should be filed and served in every application:

a. In the event that P is to be transferred from a psychiatric hospital to an acute hospital for her obstetric care, a care plan from the Mental Health Trust for that transfer, to include

i. when and, if not at a defined time, the circumstances in which P is to be transferred;

ii. the form of transport (ambulance, secure taxi etc.);

iii. which members of staff are to accompany P;

iv. an assessment of the prospects of P not co-operating with the transfer;

v. whether any specialist advice has been obtained in relation to the restraint of pregnant women and, if it has, the nature of that advice;

vi. the plans for any restraint that may be used to facilitate the transfer, including who is to undertake the restraint, at whose direction, and with a description of the techniques to be used;

vii. a clear description of what P's status will be under the MHA during transfer and whilst at the acute hospital.

b. A care plan from the Acute Trust for P's obstetric care, including:

    i.   the obstetric interventions and care that are proposed;

    ii. what anaesthesia is planned, or may be required;

    iii. when, where and by whom the interventions, care and anaesthesia are to be delivered;

    iv. what further interventions may become necessary and in what circumstances.

c. A care plan from the Acute Trust relating to the issue of restraint at the acute hospital, including:

    i.   an assessment of the prospects of P not complying with the obstetric interventions and care that is proposed;

    ii. in a stepwise and escalating fashion, a description of the measures and techniques to be used;

    iii. who is to undertake the physical or chemical restraint;

    iv. whether any specialist advice in relation to the restraint of pregnant women has been obtained and, if so, the nature of that advice.

d. A witness statement from P's responsible clinician (or to the extent that he/she cannot deal with the issues, from others) which:

    i.   contains an overview of P's psychiatric history;

    ii. details the liaison between the psychiatric and obstetric teams caring for P;

    iii. includes a focused assessment of P's capacity to consent to the obstetric treatment which is proposed;

    iv. sets out the duration for which P's lack of capacity is likely to persist despite any steps that can reasonably be taken to help her regain capacity;

    v. contains an assessment of the prospects of P not co-operating with the obstetric care that is proposed and its alternatives;

    vi. endorses the plan for transfer and any restraint during it;

    vii. compares the impact upon her mental health of the proposed obstetric treatment and restraint and any alternatives;

    viii. assesses what obstetric treatment is in P's best interests from a psychiatric perspective.

e. A witness statement from a consultant obstetrician (or to the extent that he/she cannot deal with the issues, from others) which:

    i.   contains an overview of P's obstetric history so far as it is known;

    ii. reviews the obstetric care already provided in the present pregnancy;

    iii. details the liaison between the obstetric and psychiatric teams caring for P;

    iv. explains what obstetric treatment and interventions are proposed;

    v. identifies what alternative management strategies exist;

    vi. deals with the anaesthesia which may be used and its risks/benefits;

    vii. refers to the obstetric care plan;

    viii. contains an assessment of the prospects of P not co-operating with the obstetric care that is proposed and its alternatives;

    ix. endorses the care plan for restraint at the acute hospital;

    x. compares the risks and benefits to P of the proposed obstetric treatment and interventions versus the alternatives and justification as to why the plan proposed is in P's best interests;

    xi. explains why the proposed obstetric treatment and interventions are in P's best interests.

f. Witness evidence, which may be contained in the witness statements from the consultant psychiatrist and obstetrician, which:

    i. sets out, insofar as they are able, P's past and present wishes and feelings and beliefs and values in relation to

      1. the pregnancy;

      2. obstetric care, including the proposed obstetric care and interventions;

      3. the importance of minimising the risk to her own health during pregnancy and delivery of her baby;

      4. the importance of maximising the prospects of safe delivery of the baby;

    ii. explains whether P knows of the application and, if not sets out the cogent reasons why P has not and should not be informed of the application;

    iii. identifies the individuals whose views should be taken into account in accordance with s.4(7) of the MCA and sets out the gist of their views as to

      1. whether the obstetric care that is proposed is in P's best interests and, if not, what care they consider would be;

      2. P's own past and present wishes and feelings and beliefs and values in relation to the matters in (i) above.

24. Any orders authorising medical intervention, restraint and/or a deprivation of liberty are, of course, permissive and not mandatory. P's capacity to make decisions and/or the need to take any of the measures authorised by the court must be kept under close review by her treating clinicians and medical professions throughout P's antenatal, perinatal and postnatal care.

Documents checklist

1. Application notice

2. Transfer care plan (where relevant)

3. Obstetric care plan

4. Restraint care plan

5. Witness statement from the responsible consultant psychiatrist

6. Witness statement from the responsible consultant obstetrician